ALICE SINK

Published by The History Press
Charleston, SC 29403
www.historypress.net

All images are from the Library of Congress.

First published 2011

Manufactured in the United States

ISBN 978.1.60949.275.5

Library of Congress Cataloging-in-Publication Data
Sink, Alice E.
Wicked Greensboro / Alice Sink.
p. cm.
Includes bibliographical references.
ISBN 978-1-60949-275-5
1. Crime--North Carolina--Greensboro--History--Anecdotes. 2. Corruption--North Carolina--Greensboro--History--Anecdotes. 3. Criminals--North Carolina--Greensboro--Biography--Anecdotes. 4. Greensboro (N.C.)--History--Anecdotes. 5. Greensboro (N.C.)--Social conditions--Anecdotes. 6. Greensboro (N.C.)--Moral conditions--Anecdotes. 7. Greensboro (N.C.)--Biography--Anecdotes. I. Title.
HV6795.G73S46 2011
364.109756'62--dc22
2011008304

Notice: The information in this book is true and complete to the best of our knowledge. It is offered without guarantee on the part of the author or The History Press. The author and The History Press disclaim all liability in connection with the use of this book.

Praise for Alice Sink's Writing

"Sink has taken her memories and channeled them into five years of research and writing that resulted in her…book *The Grit Behind the Miracle*, which chronicles the true story of the Infantile Paralysis Hospital that was built in 54 hours in 1944."
—Jill Doss-Raines, *Lexington Dispatch*

"Throughout the rare glimpses from 1900 to around the early 1950's, Sink stuck to one consistent theme in *Kernersville.* Sink portrayed…the sense of community."
—Brandon Keel, *Kernersville News*

"*Boarding House Reach* reminds us of one of the most important truths of life: There are no ordinary people! Every story here is fascinating—and every one importantly belongs to history."
—Fred Chappell

"Community abounds in a colorful new book about the history of North Carolina boarding houses—a traveler's guide to a lost place that was small-town and worldly at the same time."
—Lorraine Ahearn, *Greensboro News & Record*

"A very highly recommended addition for academic and community library collections, *Boarding House Reach* could serve as a template for similar studies for other states."
—Midwest Book Review

"*Hidden History of the Piedmont Triad* recounts a number of interesting stories from throughout the Triad—from historic people and places to lesser-known colorful slices of life."
—Jimmy Tomlin, *High Point Enterprise*

"[In *Hidden History of the Piedmont Triad*] Sink writes about Lexington's downtown dime stores. She describes how each counter was like a different department of the store, with a candy counter and comic book

sections popular with children…and makeup counters that carried old-fashioned items such as Tangee lipstick and Evening in Paris perfume."
—Vikki Broughton Hodges, *Dispatch*

"Did you know that a nightclub in High Point once hosted the likes of Ella Fitzgerald and Duke Ellington? Have you heard the story of Lexington native John Andrew Roman, put to death on circumstantial evidence, or the local World War II fighter plane pilot who flew eighty-two missions to prevent German fighters from attacking American bombers? These are but three of the many little-known stories…found in *Hidden History of the Piedmont Triad*."
—Arbor Lamplighter

"[*Hidden History of the Piedmont Triad*]…covers people, places and events that have been forgotten."
—Ryan Gay, lifestyles editor, *Kernersville News*

"In *Hidden History of the Piedmont Triad*, author Alice Sink rediscovers the quirky stories of the Piedmont Triad…tying North Carolina into the rest of world history."
—*Our State Magazine*

"*Hidden History of Hilton Head* offers a lively array of historical tidbits and tales. From beautiful poems written by renowned locals to the songs that guided the slaves to freedom and time-tested regional recipes, author Alice Sink's collection truly encompasses the spirit of the Lowcountry.
—The History Press (Charleston, SC)

"The premise of *No [Wo]man Is an Island* is outstanding! I laughed out loud—even hollered a few times…don't remember doing that since *Raney* and *Walking Across Egypt*. I can see it as a TV sit-com if the PC police wouldn't kill it."
—Carol Branard

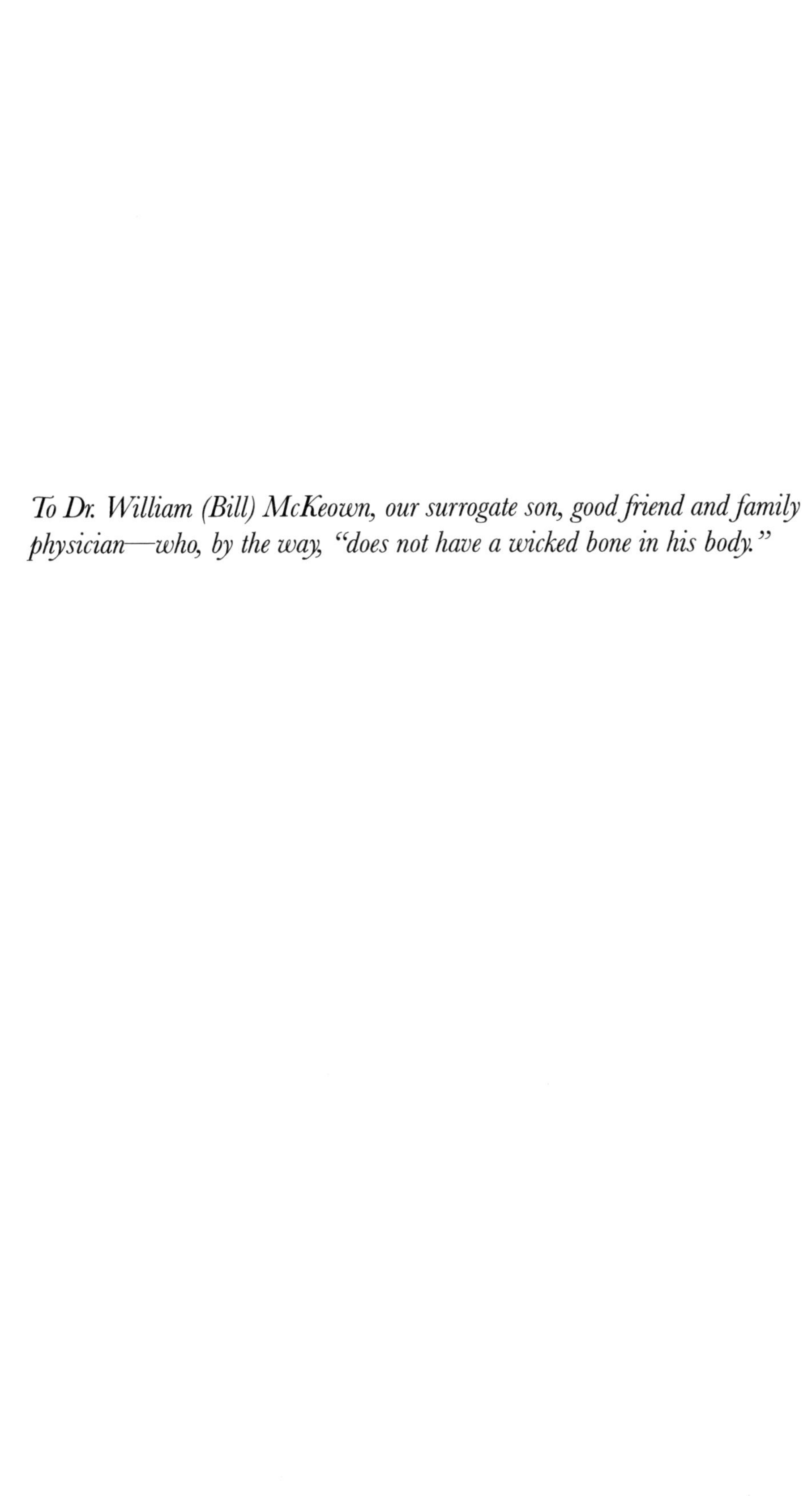

To Dr. William (Bill) McKeown, our surrogate son, good friend and family physician—who, by the way, "does not have a wicked bone in his body."

Contents

Part V. Naughty in a Playful Way

Part VI. Factories, Mills and Businesses

Preface

An unknown local writer of the 1880s recaptured something of life and customs in Greensboro before the Civil War. He writes a wickedly (showing great skill) glorified account of the "perfect life":

> [Looking back] *to the time when a few* [gas] *lamps, secured on top of posts, one to each block, lighted Greensboro on those nights when the moon refused to shine; when pony phaetons, or the family coach and a few sweetheart buggies were the means of transportation; when small negro boys were kept busy running to and fro bearing notes of invitation, of condolence, of congratulation, and perchance of love before the days of the telephone; when housemaids or butlers were sent to neighbors and friends across town laden with baskets and waiters of flowers—messages of love and friendship; when maidens as well as matrons were never seen on the street after sunset without an arm secure within that of her manly escort; when matrons could be distinguished from girls by their subdued and dignified dress; when the girls themselves wore dresses from four to six yards wide and always long enough to reach the toes of their slippers; when neatly braided coiled hair was the fashion after sixteen years of age; when men were called dudes…and wore their trousers skin tight, the upper lip adorned with cute mustachios and twirled their canes as they walked down the streets; when competent and faithful cooks ruled the*

> *kitchen; when a Smithfield ham, a 10-pound roast, and a turkey were placed upon the same dinner table on Sundays when company came; when all good sermons took one hour and often an hour and a half for delivery; when people went to visit each other instead of calling; when ladies were never seen on Main Street save when compelled to shop; when every winter brought snow about Thanksgiving time and from then until March save for intervals for a week, perhaps, there was plenty of snow to make coasting down College Hill the joy of children by day and the delight of grown folks by night; when the elm trees on West Market Street formed a veritable vista, the branches overhead interwoven into fretwork, through which the sun made wonderful patterns on the graveled street below; when Elm was really Elm Street, shady and beautiful; when Church Street was a winding road and North Elm Street stopped in front of the O. Henry Hotel; when South Greensboro was the home of half a dozen old families and only a handful of houses were seen beyond Greensboro College.*

Greensboro and its people have always been good to me. I have family and friends living there. I attended Girls' State there many, many years ago and was even elected lieutenant governor. I received both my undergraduate and graduate school education at UNCG, studying with excellent professors and acclaimed writers Fred Chappell, Lee Zacharias and Arturo Vivante. Today, I present programs and have book signings for Greensboro businesses and book and civic clubs. So, my personal perception of the city is positive; however, as is the case in all places, history does sometimes rear its wicked little head, and when it does, chilling—but true—stories are revealed.

I think it is extremely important to reconnect with the various dictionary definitions of "wicked":

> *Morally bad or wrong: acting or done with evil intent; depraved; iniquitous; Generally bad, painful, unpleasant, etc. but without any moral considerations involved (a wicked blow on the head); Naughty in a playful way; mischievous; Slang: Showing great skill (he plays a wicked game of golf).*
>
> *—Webster's New World Dictionary, Second College Edition*

Acknowledgements and Contributors

Once again, many thanks to my husband, Tom, who continues to offer suggestions and proofread my manuscripts. I truly appreciate my History Press editor, Jessica Berzon, who always kept me headed on the right track while I was researching and writing this book. Her editorial advice is priceless. Katie Parry and Dan Watson, my publicists, work diligently to arrange presentations and book signings, and I sincerely appreciate their continued efforts and publicity. For Jamie Brooke Barreto, sales specialist, let me assure you that your marketing skills are superior, and for that talent, I am grateful.

For the High Point University Smith Library folks, who helped me find necessary research materials through Interlibrary Loan and who helped me access places on the Web that I never dreamed were there, thank you: David, Mike, Bob and Nita. You never ran away when you saw me entering the library!

I also wish to acknowledge all those real southern folks who, unbeknownst to them, gave me inspiration, ideas, tidbits and specifics concerning wicked Greensboro.

Finally, on another positive note, I want to thank all those Greensboro people who, through great efforts and sacrifices, helped "right the wrongs."

PART I
Public Wrath

Daniel Worth: Imprisoned for Incendiary Doctrines

In November 1859, Daniel Worth, an abolition emissary, was accused of "inculcating, publicly and privately, his incendiary doctrines and the time has come when he should be compelled to abandon his work...We are authorized by a prominent member of the large and highly respectable family which bears the same name and to which he is distantly related to announce that they have no sympathy with the man and sternly discountenance his proceedings." This is what happened:

> *Daniel Worth was a Wesleyan Methodist preacher in Greensboro. When the* Presbyterian *called for his arrest in November, 1859, a warrant was sworn out against him on the specific charge of circulating Helper's* Impending Crisis. *On December 22, he gave himself up and the sheriff committed him to the Guilford County jail where he remained four months awaiting trial, denied, as all prisoners in the State were at this time, the ordinary comforts of life so that, during the severely inclement winter, his feet froze and his health became very feeble. Later, five of his converts were also arrested. Crowds surrounded the jail in Greensboro where Worth was imprisoned, and it was sometimes*

A pillory.

> *feared that he might be lynched. In January, 1860, charges were preferred against him in Randolph County, and in March he was tried in Asheboro, found guilty, and sentenced to imprisonment for a year, the mildest punishment possible under the incendiary publications act. Late in April his trial came up in Greensboro, where he was again found guilty and sentenced to imprisonment. Later the Supreme Court upheld the decision, and Worth, rather than submit to imprisonment which would have endangered his life, left the State.*

At the next session of the legislature, anyone circulating "incendiary documents" or "exciting" a Negro to "a spirit of insurrection" was declared guilty of a felony, and anyone using "inflammatory language" was made guilty of a misdemeanor.

Although laws against mayhem had been passed in 1754 and in 1791, a more stringent measure was enacted in 1831. Punishment for the first offense of malicious maiming was a sentence of two hours in the pillory and thirty-nine lashes on the bare back, while for the second it was death without benefit of clergy, explained here:

> *Although the term* without the benefit of clergy *is used colloquially today to describe a couple living together outside a legal marriage, originally members of the clergy were exempted from capital punishment upon conviction of particular crimes based on this privilege, but it did not encompass crimes of either high treason or misdemeanors. Furthermore,* benefit of clergy *existed to alleviate the severity of criminal laws as applied to the clergy. It was, however, found to promote such extensive abuses that it was ultimately eliminated. Interestingly, clergy were not the only ones to benefit, but the exemption was extended to all persons for all crimes, except high treason.*

Maiming without malice was punishable by fine and six months' imprisonment. Throughout the period, indictments for assault and battery far outnumbered all other offenses tried in the county counts. In antebellum days, dueling was the most honorable method of settling a quarrel.

Camp meetings.

Camp meetings were popular religious events. Bodily contortions occurred: "clinched fists, limbs thrown into almost every imaginable position, and the hair of women would crack like a whip." Not everyone, however, was religiously moved: "On the contrary, there was scoffing, ridicule, and open defiance of the meetings by some. There were liquor peddling, drunkenness, and other abuses. And there were those who chose to look upon the camp gatherings as a sort of entertainment—'tares among the wheat.'"

ADAM CROOKS: DRAGGED FROM THE PULPIT AND JAILED

A great many in North Carolina were rankling over the terms of the Compromise of 1850. In May, the antislavery associations met in New York to review the accomplishments of the year. The *North Carolina Standard* ran a report declaring that a Wesleyan Methodist missionary had been laboring with much success for a year in Guilford County. The *Standard* recommended that the missionary be found and that "the people take him in hand, in open day, and compel him to leave the country":

> *The missionary was Adam Crooks, who, in response to a request from a group of Guilford County Methodists who were dissatisfied with the stand taken on slavery by the Methodist Episcopal South. Two years later Jesse McBride joined him, and together they ministered unto the growing number of Wesleyan Methodist congregations and openly preached "the strange doctrines of the abolitionists in the land of the bleeding slave." Both were young men, gentle and mild-mannered, preaching against slavery in a section which had long heard anti-slavery sentiment expressed. They had come to win converts to the Wesleyan Methodist faith and to preach the whole doctrine of their creed which also included strictures against the use of spirituous liquor and membership in secret organizations. They preached nearly every day and won a convert at nearly every sermon. Soon their activities came under the suspicion of religious denominations which disapproved of proselytizing, slaveholders*

Southern ideas of liberty.

who feared that their laborers would be disturbed, farmers who habitually distilled their crops, and lodge members who resented the implication that a fraternal order was ungodly.

In May, 1850, when the North Carolina Standard *ordered the men to run out of the State, there were many willing to lend a hand. At the time, McBride probably had already been arrested, and Crooks' arrest soon followed. Their trial came up at the October term of the Superior Count. Before "a large crowd of anxious spectators," the court found the evidence against McBride to be that he had handed the small daughter of a certain Washington Kennedy an incendiary pamphlet,* The Ten Commandments. *Despite the cry on the street for hanging, the jury acquitted Crooks, but found McBride guilty, and the court ordered that he receive twenty lashes on the bare back, stand an hour in the pillory, and be imprisoned in the county jail for a year. "Good—very good!" exclaimed the* Standard. *"We wish the law could take hold of their necks, instead of their backs." The Register thought that "nothing but that high sense of loyalty to the law" saved McBride "from summary punishment." The missionaries were also indicted in Guilford County, but the grand jury failed to find a true bill against them.*

The public wrath now focused on Crooks. In June, he was dragged from the pulpit and taken to jail, where he remained for three days until he agreed as the price of his release not to preach again. Many thought that his agreement was to leave the state, and when he continued preaching, his enemies were determined to be rid of him. Finally Crooks realized that his own life and the lives of his converts were endangered. He left; all was still not calm:

> *For a while, after the McBride and Crooks episode, the papers let abolition and the free Negroes alone. It was not until November, 1859, the* Presbyterian *again gave news of the abolition missionary in the State. Without disclosing the name of the man, the editor declared that an agent of the Boston Tract Society was at work in North Carolina. "Society must be protected against cut-throats and assassins," the Presbyterian declared, "and the sword of the civil magistrate is the instrument which God has appointed for their punishment. The agent of the Boston Tract Society is an abolition emissary...The mildest treatment which can be administered to him is to remove him from the State, and this is what we advised." A cry immediately*

Slavery is dead.

went up for the name of the agent, and a month later the Presbyterian gave out the name of Daniel Worth. "For a year or two past, it is notorious that he has been inculcating, publicly and privately, his incendiary doctrines in Randolph and Guilford counties, and the time has come when he should be compelled to abandon his work...We are authorized by a prominent member of the large and highly respectable family which bears the same name and to which he is distantly related...to announce that they have no sympathy with the man and sternly discountenance his proceedings."

Quakers: Bear Arms or Pay the Tax!

In 1742, when William Peckover, a Quaker, visited North Carolina, he found five meetinghouses in an area of thirty miles and "many solid, weighty, good Friends." Six or seven hundred persons attended these meetings, and there were nine or ten persons gifted in ministry, with

Early Quaker meetinghouse and school.

more developing. New Garden, begun about 1750 in Guilford County, soon became the most important Quaker settlement in North Carolina. The Revolution seriously interrupted the growth of the Society of Friends and brought the society into disrepute because its members would not actively support the war. Many youths of the society joined the army despite the fact that they were promptly disowned. The nineteenth century opened, therefore, with the public mind prejudiced against the Quakers.

In addition to the fact that they were a "peculiar sect" that practiced "plainness in gesture, speech, apparel and furniture of houses," they had not helped to win the Revolution. They did not attend militia musters. In 1804, a bill came up in the House of Commons proposing that Quakers be required to pay a double poll tax because of their exemption from militia service.

The bill was defeated on its first reading, but each year the question of "giving a hereditary privilege to a particular set of men" became more acute until in 1830 the legislature actually passed a law requiring Quakers either to bear arms or to pay a tax of $2.50.

EMIGRATION: ANTEBELLUM SLUR

It is difficult to estimate the exact population that North Carolina lost in the antebellum period, but certainly its people were on the move southward and northwestward from the opening of the century. In 1818, Governor Branch urged the legislature to adopt measures at once "to arrest the progress of emigration" and make "our citizens contented and happy to remain at home." Still the stream of emigration continued. In 1845, the *Greensborough Patriot* recorded: "On last Tuesday morning nineteen carts, with about one hundred persons, passed this place, from Wake County, on their way to the West. And thus they have been going almost every day from the lower counties."

By 1820, North Carolina had been popularly dubbed "the Boeotia of America" or "the second Nazareth." Archibald D. Murphey, discouraged by repeated failures to steer the General Assembly to a liberal state policy, described the spirit of North Carolina as "radically mean and groveling."

"The Mass of the Common People in the Country," he said, "are lazy, sickly, poor, dirty and ignorant." It is undoubtedly true that emigration took from Greensboro many of its best citizens and left behind the reactionary and the conservative.

Equality Reigns over Wickedness: The Greensboro Four Sit-ins

If anyone came into my store and tried to stop business, I'd throw him out. The Negro should behave himself and show he's a good citizen.
—Former President Harry S. Truman

In January 1960, North Carolina Agricultural and Technical College (A&T) student Ezell Blair Jr. returned to Greensboro from his Christmas holiday in Wilmington. When he arrived at Union Bus Station, he was hungry from his long trip. Because he was black, he was not allowed to sit down and eat at the bus station's lunch counter.

Separate drinking fountains.

In Greensboro during this time, this custom was not unusual. Although many people, led by Reverend Martin Luther King Jr., had protested successfully against segregation in schools and on buses, many private businesses had not yet been challenged.

> **Jim Crow Laws**—*These were state and local laws made between 1876 and 1965, mostly in the South. These laws segregated people by race in restaurants, hotels, restrooms, and most other public accommodations. The phrase "Jim Crow" came from an 1828 song and dance, "Jump Jim Crow," written and sung by a white theater entertainer who blackened his face with burnt cork and dressed as a slave.*

By 1960, side-by-side water fountains—one for whites and one for blacks—had gradually disappeared. Also gone were separate public

"Me and Jim." Little nude black girl with mandolin sitting on limb with crow.

Cartoon: "Jim Crow."

bathrooms. Lunch counters with stools were still for whites only. African Americans could not sit down to eat. They had to stand.

Ezell Blair Jr. did not understand this law. When he returned to his A&T dormitory that night, he and his roommate, David Richmond, were joined by two other students, Franklin McCain and Joseph McNeil. They all talked about segregation at lunch counters in privately owned businesses. Blair told his three friends that he did not know why blacks were not allowed to sit down and eat in public places. He thought it was time for a big change.

Ezell Blair's friends said that they felt the same way, but all anybody seemed to do was *talk* about change. They wondered why everybody just walked away after they had been refused sit-down service. The four young men were afraid that nothing would ever change in the South if all blacks did was talk. It seemed there was lots of *talk, talk, talk* from both parents and college officials—but no action.

Historical facts influenced these Greensboro teenagers to act on their beliefs. Each had probably heard of the lynching of Emmett Till, a fourteen-year-old Mississippi boy who was accused of whistling at a white woman. In the middle of the night, a group of men beat and shot Emmett, tied a seventy-five-pound cotton gin fan around his neck and then threw him in the river. None of the men was found guilty in a court of law.

No doubt, the four A&T students had also heard of other disturbing events. Charlotte, North Carolina high school student Dorothy Geraldine Counts, in 1957, had been pelted with sticks and stones by a crowd of white students after she enrolled in Harding High School. Also in 1957, a crowd of students, sightseers and the press waited outside Central High School in Little Rock, Arkansas, opposing the admission of African American students. Two years later, in 1959, African American students Elizabeth Eckford, Jefferson Thomas and seven others were denied entry by the Arkansas National Guard to all-white Central High in Little Rock, Arkansas. They entered successfully eleven days later, escorted by the 101st Airborne.

Perhaps these young men had vivid memories of Duke Ellington and band members playing baseball in front of their segregated motel in 1955. Then, there were Ku Klux Klan activities. In 1960, the four young men in their A&T dormitory knew that action was needed before any changes would be made. They decided they would stage a sit-in at the all-white Woolworth's lunch counter on South Elm Street in Greensboro. This store was selected for several reasons.

First, they knew that Woolworth stores in other areas of the country served blacks at their lunch counters. Second, they knew that the Greensboro Woolworth's had only white waitresses. Black workers cooked and cleaned. Third, they did not like Woolworth's double standard. After all, why could blacks spend their money shopping in the rest of the store but could not sit at the lunch counter? They had to eat at the stand-up snack bar or bakery counter.

Their plans made, the group decided to meet at A&T State's Bluford Library in mid-afternoon the next day. They slept little the rest of that night. All went to their college classes. At 3:00 p.m., they met for their walk up East Market Street. They passed through the railroad underpass that separated the black and white communities of Greensboro.

Some accounts say that McCain, a ROTC member, wore his uniform simply because he had not had time to change clothes after his last class. A picture taken later that afternoon shows a knee-length coat covering what may have been military clothing. He is wearing what looks like a military hat.

Through the years since that February 1, 1960 day, other different stories have been told about the events that followed. One account says that walking four abreast, the teenagers passed Ralph Johns's small downtown clothing store. Mr. Johns was on the sidewalk and overheard them talking about going to Woolworth's to start a sit-in. He then went inside and telephoned Jo Spivey, a reporter for the *Record*, Greensboro's afternoon paper, to tell her what they had said. Perhaps that did happen.

Then, there is Miles Wolff's book entitled *Lunch at the Five and Ten: The Greensboro Sit-Ins*, which gives a different slant. According to Wolff, the four A&T students entered Ralph Johns's store and Mr. Johns said to McNeil, "Well, I thought I'd never see you again." McNeil answered, "I told you I'd be back."

Wolff writes about all four of the young men going to the back of the store, where Johns coached them on what they should do and say when they got to Woolworth's. He even had them practice in front of him. He gave them money to buy items when they got to the five and dime store. He also told them to be sure to get receipts for everything they bought.

Johns promised he would pay their legal fees and bail them out of jail—if they were arrested. And one more thing: they should never let anyone know he had anything to do with helping them. He did not want to be called by his real name but, rather, referred to as "Number One." McNeil would become "Number Two," Blair "Number Three," McCain "Number Four" and Richmond "Number Five." Maybe this version of the story is the correct one. Only the people involved know for sure.

Today, when people talk about the 1960 sit-ins, they give different reasons why Ralph Johns got involved with the four A&T students and their mission. Rarely do folks agree. Some say he simply wanted to get more African American business for his clothing store. Others feel Johns was a man who had big dreams of becoming famous, and this was how he chose to do that. Still others believe he really wanted to fight segregation. Maybe his motive was a combination of all three. We do not know.

One fact is certain. After the four young men left Ralph Johns's clothing store, they turned onto South Elm Street at Jefferson Square. They stopped suddenly when they saw the red Woolworth's sign with gold lettering looming ahead. The four talked for a few minutes about what might happen after they got back to campus. They knew they might be expelled, beat up or hauled off to jail. However, after discussing everything that might happen, they all continued to walk down the sidewalk.

After they went inside Woolworth's, they split up in pairs and went to different counters in the store. They bought small items such as toothpaste, combs, pencils, notebooks and erasers. Their purchases proved to them that blacks could be served anywhere in the store—except sitting on a stool at the all-white lunch counter.

The long, L-shaped stainless steel lunch counter with plastic cushioned stools took up almost two walls of the store's first floor and could seat sixty-six customers. About a dozen white people were enjoying their coffee breaks. McNeil and McCain were the first two to sit. Blair and Richmond joined them.

The "Colored Only" and "White Only" signs had been removed from the store about three years earlier when Greensboro tennis counts and libraries had been integrated. Geneva Tisdale, a black woman cleaning behind the counter, thought that the boys were from out of town and didn't know the ways of Greensboro. She said, in a newspaper interview, "I just thought there was somebody here from someplace else that didn't know they didn't serve blacks, so I kept on doing what I was doing."

According to author Miles Wolff, the following conversation took place:

> *A white waitress stood before the boys. "I'm sorry. We don't serve Negroes here," she stated. They refused to leave. Ezell Blair said, "I beg to disagree with you. You just finished serving me at a counter only two feet away from here." The waitress motioned towards the stand-up counter and said, "Negroes eat at the other end." "What do you mean? This is a public place, isn't it? If it isn't, then why don't you sell membership cards? If you do that, then I'll understand that this is a private concern."*
>
> *The waitress said, "Well, you won't get any service here!" and walked away. The boys did not budge. Then an African American*

> *female who worked at the steam table behind the counter, assured the four young men that they would not be served at the all-white sit-down lunch counter. When they still would not go away, the girl said, "You're acting stupid, ignorant! That's why we can't get anywhere today. You know you're supposed to eat at the other end."*

Another African American who was washing dishes behind the counter "was heard to shout at them that they were 'stupid, ignorant, rabble-rousers, troublemakers.'" All four young men stayed where they were.

Later, a male African American worker tried to get the boys to go. "Don't be troublemakers," he urged. "You're just hurting race relations by sitting there."

Next, the balding manager of Woolworth's, Clarence "Curley" Harris, talked to the four. When they still would not budge, Harris summoned his supervisor, who said, "They'll soon give up. Leave, and be forgotten."

Harris probably did not think this would happen, so he left the store and walked two blocks to the police station. There, the chief of police, Paul Calhoun, told him that nothing could be done if the boys were behaving appropriately. Calhoun did send an officer to the store—just in case.

Before Harris and the policeman returned, an elderly white woman who had been watching their sit-in walked up to the four young men. "Boys," she said, "I am just so proud of you. My only regret is that you didn't do this ten or fifteen years ago."

That compliment, no doubt, gave the boys pride. What if they had done this when they had been eight or ten years old? It was something for them to think about.

Back from the police station, Harris announced that the store would be closing early. He locked the front door. The boys stayed at the counter for about fifteen more minutes. Then they filed out quietly through a side entrance. They had not been served food or drink. According to Miles Wolff, one of the boys called over his shoulder, "I'll be back tomorrow."

Outside the store, *Record* photographer Jack Moebes got a picture of the students walking four abreast. In this famous photograph, none of the young men wore military clothing. On the way back to campus, McCain said, "I've never felt so good in my life. I truly felt I had my going-to-the-mountain experience."

A recruitment meeting that night back at A&T produced a few more students interested in the sit-in. The next day, Tuesday, February 2, more students went back to the Woolworth's lunch counter, arriving about ten o'clock. Reports here also differ. Some say as few as six students went; others say as many as thirty-one participated. Again, certain facts are true: First, the students, dressed in coats and ties, sat quietly at the counter and read books or studied. Second, no one approached them and asked them to leave. And third, they were not served. According to Wolff, "Occasionally a student would ask a waitress, 'Miss, may I have something?' but that was the extent of the confrontation."

Interviewed by Marvin Sykes, a Greensboro *Record* staff writer, Franklin McCain and Ezell Blair acted as spokesmen for the group, saying they were prepared to keep on coming for "several days, several weeks… until something is done." Ezell Blair issued this statement for the *Record*: "Negro adults have been complacent and fearful. It is time for someone to wake up and change the situation…and we decided to start here."

When a reporter asked Manager Harris for a statement, he said, "They can just sit there. It's nothing to me." J.W. Largen, the district superintendent of Woolworth's, added this comment: "We haven't refused anybody. Our girls have been busy and they couldn't get around to everybody."

At 12:30 p.m., the students left Woolworth's and did not return. The afternoon Greensboro *Record* second section headline read: "A&T Students Launch Sit-Down Demand for Service at Downtown Lunch Counter." After the wire service picked up the story, news spread quickly to college campuses as far away as New York.

When A&T students talked with the president of their college, Dr. Warmoth T. Gibbs, and told him that students were staging a sit-in at Woolworth's, Dr. Gibbs acted surprised and commented that Woolworth's "did not have a reputation for fine food." He referred the matter to the dean of the college, William C. Gamble, who said, "Let them sit."

On Tuesday night, February 2, A&T students, college officials and men from the Greensboro store met. They asked if Woolworth's would pay their way for them to travel to the regional office in Atlanta, Georgia. Their request was denied, so, according to Wolff, that same night they wrote a letter to the head office in New York:

> *Dear Mr. President:*
> *We, the undersigned are students at the Negro college in the city of Greensboro. Time and time again we have gone into Woolworth stores of Greensboro. We have bought thousands of items at hundreds of the counters in your store. Our money being accepted without rancor or discrimination and with politeness toward us. When at a long counter just three feet away our money is not acceptable because of the color of our skins. This letter is not being written with resentment toward your company, but with a hope of understanding... We are asking that your company take a firm stand to eliminate discrimination. We firmly believe that God will give courage and guidance in the solving of this problem.*

By the third day, Wednesday, February 3, 1960, the *Daily News* published a short piece under the headline "Negroes Fail to Obtain Service."

A total of eighty-five white and black students from local colleges joined the Woolworth's sit-in on Wednesday about 11:00 a.m. to fill sixty-three of the sixty-six seats, with others waiting in the aisles. Everything had been peaceful and quiet—up to this point. At 1:30 p.m., an argument broke out, so the police escorted those involved from the store. Later that afternoon Woolworth's closed the stand-up counter that had in the past served only African Americans.

Malcolm Seawell, North Carolina attorney general, issued a statement saying that "he knew of no law that would force a private business to serve anybody it did not want to." A&T officials responded by saying the college "could not restrict students' outside activities."

On Thursday, the fourth day of the sit-ins, the local morning paper, the *Daily News*, carried a story and picture. One student at A&T wrote in the college newspaper his experience:

> *After attending a mass meeting in Harrison Auditorium, I was... inspired to go down to Woolworth's and just sit hoping to be served... The doors opened and in we went. I almost ran because I was determined to get a seat and I was very much interested in being the first to sit down. I sat down and there was a waitress standing directly in front of me, so I asked her if I might have a cup of black coffee and two donuts please. She looked at me and moved to another area of the counter.*

According to one account, tension was running pretty high by Thursday, when some three hundred blacks arrived—to be met by at least that many white boys, who took all the lunch counter stools. The police report for this day read: "During the mid-morning, a white boy spilled a glass of coke on the head of a colored student. We are unable to say whether it was accidental or intentionally." African American students left Woodworth's and walked to S.H. Kress & Company about half a block away. There, they sat at Kress basement lunch counter amid policemen and detectives.

Friday, February 5, 1960, turned out to be an almost identical repeat of the day before. Both black and white students arrived at both variety stores. The police report noted: "There was a great deal of pushing and shoving between the colored and white students as they walked in the aisles." What had begun a few days earlier as a quiet, peaceful sit-in became rowdy.

Back at A&T on Friday, the student newspaper, the *Register*, published interviews with those involved in the sit-ins. The editor wrote: "The time has indeed come when we must all face up to the facts, and realize that America cannot continue its present position of leadership in world affairs with the stigma of race prejudice and discrimination on the one hand, and grin-on-the-face tactics on the other. The season is here now."

Saturday, February 6, 1960, an unseasonably warm day, brought local shoppers to the downtown area. Reports indicate that by mid-morning, about six hundred people crowded around the Woolworth's lunch counter. White boys waved Confederate flags, and African Americans carried small American flags. The aisles soon became clogged. Someone threw a firecracker, another shot a water pistol and others were arrested for fighting and being drunk. When the A&T football team made its appearance at noon, tension rose to its highest level.

Then, at 1:09 p.m., J.W. Largen from the regional office answered the telephone at Woolworth's in Greensboro, and a female voice told him that there was a bomb in the basement. At that time, Manager Harris climbed onto one of the counters and announced that everyone must leave the store. No one left, so two policemen joined Harris on the counter and ordered immediate evacuation. This time, people left in a hurry. The police found no bomb, but the store remained closed the remainder of

Saturday. When students were forced to leave Woolworth's that day, they walked a couple of blocks down the street to S.H. Kress & Co.

The police report indicates the chaos that followed: "Tensions were very high. Silverware such as knives, forks, and spoons was in evidence in possession of both colored and white when the manager announced that the store was closed [in the interest of public safety]. There was evidence of relief on both the colored and the white."

At about 3:30 p.m., editor H.W. Kendall of the *Daily News* received a telephone call from Governor Luther H. Hodges, who wanted to know if he should send National Guard troops to Greensboro. Kendall asked if the mayor, chief of police or city manager had made that request. Because they had not, the governor decided not to send the guard.

That night, A&T students held a meeting on campus and agreed to call a two-week truce. Mayor George Roach expressed his belief that there would be an honorable solution.

The *Daily News* headline on Sunday read: "A&T Students Call Two-Week Recess in Protest Here."

By mid-February, students in eleven southern cities had staged sit-ins. They went not only to Woolworth stores in their area but also targeted another dime store chain, S.H. Kress.

After several days of sit-ins, black female worker Geneva Tisdale, who was expecting a baby, was afraid that the KKK would come into the store, so Rachel Holt, the lunch counter manager, sent Tisdale upstairs. Finally, because of the sit-ins, the lunch counter was shut down.

Picket lines formed along South Elm and Sycamore Streets. "Don't shop at Woodworth's" the signs urged. City officials met to discuss everything that had happened and tried to come to some kind of compromise. Ed Zane and Spencer Love, Burlington Mill executives, were determined that race violence would not happen in Greensboro. They were probably the ones who actually got Woolworth's to agree to integrate. It took another five months before African Americans were served at Woolworth's lunch counter.

As in most major events, irony plays an important part, and the Woolworth sit-ins were no exception. The Greensboro Four—as they were now called—would not have the honor of eating the first meal at the newly integrated lunch counter. On July 25, 1960, Geneva Tisdale and two other female kitchen workers, all wearing their best clothes, were the first African Americans served at Woolworth's sit-down lunch counter. Tisdale had an egg salad sandwich and soda.

"It was a good sandwich," Tisdale told the press. "I know because I made it myself!" Years later, she was heard to say, "They never knew that it was Woolworth girls that was the first to sit at the counter to be served after they opened it up."

It was all over. The next day, the *Daily News* printed a one-page column with no pictures. After that, news of the sit-ins was scarce.

The Greensboro Four returned to their studies at A&T. These four teenagers had sparked an important movement throughout the South. One journalist explains this wildfire effect: "Black students in colleges throughout the South said, 'What's wrong with us? Why don't we go out and do the same thing?'"

Other African American students, who started protests in various other southern states, vowed to obey several unwritten rules. They dressed in their best clothes, sat quietly and read or studied and left every other stool vacant so that any white person could join the cause. Sit-ins spread from lunch counters to integration of all public places. Students made a pledge not to accept bail if they were jailed. They decided to stay behind bars to show how serious they were about their cause.

One of the first steps to erase racial inequality and injustice in the South came after students, churches, civil rights organizations and citizens became active in changing Woolworth's company policy of not serving blacks at its lunch counter. By summer, lunch counters and restaurants in thirty-three southern cities had become integrated. By August 1960, an estimated seventy thousand people had participated in sit-ins in both the North and South.

THE GREENSBORO MASSACRE

Willena Cannon, a lifelong civil rights activist and member of the Workers Viewpoint Organization, helped arrange a "Death to the Klan" rally and conference. What is now known as the Greensboro massacre occurred on November 3, 1979, when five protest marchers were shot and killed by members of the Ku Klux Klan and the American Nazi Party. Reflections, remembrances and emotions differ concerning this event, but one fact is certain—five people were killed and ten others wounded:

> *The marchers killed were: Sandi Smith, a nurse and civil rights activist; Dr. James Waller, president of a local textile workers union who ceased medical practice to organize workers; Bill Sampson, a graduate of the Harvard School of Divinity; Cesar Cauce, a Cuban immigrant who graduated* magna cum laude *from Duke University; and Dr. Michael Nathan chief of pediatrics at Lincoln Community Health Center in Durham, North Carolina, a clinic that helped children from low-income families. Gunshots wounded ten others.*

Author Sally Avery Bermanzohn, whose husband, Paul, was shot in the head and the arm, permanently paralyzing his left side, has written extensively about her perception of that day:

> *On November 3, 1979, Ku Klux Klansmen and American Nazis opened fire on union organizers and civil rights activists in Greensboro, North Carolina, killing five close friends of mine. We were black and white radical activists who had deep roots in the civil rights, Black Power, antiwar, and women's liberation movements. In the 1970s we became union organizers in textile mills and hospitals. Many of us, myself included, were members of the Communist Workers Party. On that fateful day, we wanted to protest the 1979 reemergence of the Ku Klux Klan (KKK) in areas of North Carolina in which union drives were in progress. We planned a spirited march through Greensboro, followed by a conference. Instead, the KKK and Nazis attacked us as we were gathering to march.*

Kathryn Watterson of *Trenton Times* takes her readers back to November 3, 1979, and Kwame Cannon's exposure to the turmoil:

> *Kwame Cannon was 10 years old the rainy November morning he went with his mother Willena Cannon to an anti–Ku Klux Klan rally outside the public housing project where they lived in Greensboro, N.C. The*

demonstration was led by Kwame's mother and her friends—leaders of an interracial group working to organize black and white factory workers at local textile mills.

"We were all singing," Kwame remembers, "when the caravan came down the street." Kwame saw the confederate flag on one of the cars and sounds he thought at first were shots from a cap gun. "They're shooting," he hollered as he began to run with his friends Ricky and Ayo.

Two television cameramen recorded the Nov. 3 bloodbath. Klansmen and Nazis parked their cars, coolly removed weapons from the trunk of a blue Ford Fairlane, took aim and shot down one unarmed demonstrator after another. A cigarette dangled casually from one Klansman's lips as he lifted, leveled and fired his shotgun. Another white supremacist sprinted down the sidewalk with a pistol in his hand, firing bullets into the neck and chest of an organizer named Cesar Cauce who already was wounded.

Watterson concludes her article with these statements:

Klansmen and American Nazis shot 13 people that day—several of them right between the eyes. Five died. Even though the video coverage showed the murders clearly, an all-white jury acquitted the Klansmen and Nazis of all charges. A civil trial eventually determined collusion between the Klan and Greensboro police in the slayings and ordered the City of Greensboro to pay damages to the widows and children of the victims. But no Klansman ever paid one penny in damages. Nor did any Klansman ever spend a day in prison for the murders—not even Dave Matthews, who admitted to police that he thought he had shot three people. "There were some innocent people shot, I recon," he said. "But I was shooting at the niggers."

According to author Sally Avery Bermanzohn, the May 26, 2006, 532-page Greensboro Truth and Reconciliation Commission Report (GTRC) is "based on thorough research of all available sources and carefully weighs sharply-conflicting testimonies":

> *The commission's findings are comprehensive. Most important, they find the police culpable for failing to provide safety for the protesters or the residents of the community where the Klan attacked. In great detail, the report describes the GPD's awareness of the Klan caravan's movements, and their failure to take action to protect people. The report's conclusion states that a majority of the commissioners believe the "among* some *in the* [Greensboro Police] *department, there was intentionality to fail to provide adequate protection," and the commissioners name six officers who were decision makers that day. The findings criticize the city's scapegoating of the victims and the failure of the court system to find the killers guilty. The commissioners also criticize us for violent language, a point with which many of the survivors agree.*

Film of the Greensboro shootings from November 3, 1979, is available on YouTube. While incomplete, such film is purported to provide documentary evidence of the crimes. After viewing the videotapes, which captured much of the action, author Signe Waller, wife of slain physician James Michael Waller, made these comments:

> *Even as the caravan was approaching the demonstrators, a camera picked up the motions of one of the attackers loading a pistol from the passenger seat of a slowly moving vehicle. When viewing the tapes, one is struck by the casual, unhurried manner in which firearms are removed from the trunk of a rear vehicle and distributed. The assailants give no indication of being concerned about possible retaliation from those attacked or about police interference with their actions. They do not bother to take cover, and they do not look behind. Striking, too, is the cigarette dangling all the while from the mouth of one of the shooters. About a half dozen of the armed intruders continued to fire on people as they ran for cover or tried to ward off the attackers with sticks.*

Paul and Sally Bermanzohn, in their book entitled *The True Story of the Greensboro Massacre*, have described what they saw in the videotapes:

> *Klansmen calmly walk to the trunks of the rear cars, open them, and take out and distribute rifles and handguns. A shot rings out and*

> *demonstrators run for cover. Armed Klansmen walk about, carefully select victims, fire and reload...They seem like casual participants at a skeet shoot. One of them methodically pumps bullets into the body of a fallen protester. Another shoots with a lit cigarette dangling from his mouth...The gunmen calmly pack their weapons in the cars and slowly drive off.*

The morning of November 3, 1979, changed the lives of many. The Klan and Nazi ambush lasted only eighty-eight seconds.

UNSOLVED MURDER

Seven-year-old Shalonda Poole disappeared from her Ashe Street home on July 20, 1990. The next day, she was found dead in a wooded area behind nearby Jones Elementary School. Shalonda had been raped and killed. News reports vary: one indicated the child was strangled to death and another that she was stabbed. Her killing remains unsolved; however, Greensboro police are now continuing their investigation, thanks to a federally funded grant in the amount of $308,000 for cold cases.

Ryan Seals, staff writer of the Greensboro *News &Record*, recalls that tragic day twenty years ago:

> *Saturday, July 21, 1990, was supposed to be a day of togetherness at the Poole family's home in the Hampton Homes community. The children were supposed to spend time with their father, Gattis, who had just been released from jail after serving 30 days on alcohol-related charges. Early that morning, about 3 or 4 a.m., Marilyn slipped into bed with her husband after completing her shift in the mailroom at the* News & Record. *They talked for a while, but Gattis had an early morning fishing trip planned with a neighbor.*
>
> *"He kept telling me not to go to sleep because the kids would be up in a minute and would be ready to eat," Marilyn recalled. Gattis left the house about 6 a.m. Marilyn dozed off after checking on the kids at 6:30 a.m. About 8:15 a.m., Shanda woke her up and said her twin Shalonda was missing. In a panic, Marilyn called neighbors...No one*

> *had seen Shalonda. A neighbor left to get Gattis, who rushed home to join the search.*
>
> *"He said, 'We are going to find her,'" Marilyn said in a recent interview.*
>
> *"I said, 'No, we aren't, because she's dead. I can feel that she's dead.'"*
>
> *A suspect, Melvin Bennett, 32, a mentally disabled man living near the Poole house, was arrested within two days. Bennett confessed; however, a psychologist said Melvin was "very susceptible to suggestion and would say anything anybody wanted him to say." Nevertheless, the confession sent Melvin to jail for a couple of years to await his trial on September 28, 1992.*
>
> *DNA testing showed that semen from the girl's body did not belong to Bennett. Police then tested four other men, including Shalonda's father; all tested negative.*

The family is still trying to heal, but that has been difficult:

> *Marilyn Poole…believes she knows who is responsible. "I just want to know why he did it," she said. "He needs to confess." After Shalonda's death, the Poole children went to counseling. Their father turned to heavy drinking and lashed out in anger. Their mother worked as many as four jobs at a time—her way of easing the pain. She had to stop when she had a nervous breakdown. Twin Shanda suffered from years of drug abuse and spent time at a mental hospital. "I kept in trouble," Shanda said, adding that she's turned her life around in recent years and rejoined her family. Family members say they cling to Shalonda's memory every day.*

Just recently, Greensboro rededicated the Shalonda Poole Park at Jones Elementary in an emotional memorial service.

PART II

Public Health and Welfare

Shortage of Medical Doctors

For a long time, there was no reliable physician in the Greensboro area. This disturbed David Caldwell, so he sent for medical books in order to teach himself how to practice medicine in the mid-1700s. Soon after, Dr. Woodsides, a relative of Mrs. Caldwell, came to Greensboro for a visit and was urged to stay. Unfortunately, he died soon after. David Caldwell studied Woodsides's medical books until he felt qualified in the late 1700s to become the town's doctor. He had no formal medical training; therefore, he did not earn a degree. He simply knew when he was qualified to serve the Greensboro community as its physician.

During the American Revolution (1775–1781), the British general Cornwallis was in Guilford County several days before fighting began, and he moved his army from farm to farm, including David Caldwell's, in order to replenish the food supply of his men. What they and their horses could not consume, they destroyed. Corncribs were pulled down, leaving the grain to rot at a time when corn was selling, in some parts, for five to twenty dollars per bushel. Hay and fodder were burned or scattered about to render it useless. This is reportedly what happened as the redcoats encamped on Caldwell's place:

> [Mrs. Caldwell] *retired to the smokehouse where she was confined for two days and nights with no other food for herself or her children than a few dried peaches, which she had chanced to have in her pockets. Her situation was particularly distressing as she had born five children in two years or a little more...two sets of twins...* [and] *a young infant. When the army moved...every panel of fence on the premises was consumed or carried away; every living thing was destroyed except one old goose.*

The last major battle of the American Revolution was fought at the county seat of Guilford. After the fighting was over, Dr. Caldwell was among those who went to the battlefield to bury the dead and to attend the sick and wounded. What happened next is recorded by historians:

> *In the McNairy house which was one of those used as a hospital, they cut off legs and arms and threw them into a cart at the door until it was pretty well loaded; and then they were taken away and buried. Along with the amputated limbs were buried the bodies of the dead—the men who gave their lives for the liberty of those who came after them.*

This self-taught method continued into the early 1800s with the next generation, David Caldwell Jr., whose medical education was as follows: "Dr. David Caldwell, Jr., received his education at home under the tutelage of his father...The case of Dr. David Caldwell M.D. [the son], seems unique in that while he never attended a course of medical lectures, he received, without application for it, a diploma from the Medical Department of the University of Pennsylvania."

Subsequently, Dr. David Caldwell Jr. practiced medicine in Greensboro for forty-five years.

QUACKERY

Definitions of quackery:

- *Medical practice and advice based on observation and experience in ignorance of scientific findings*

- *Charlatanism: the dishonesty of a charlatan*
- *Quackery is a derogatory term used to describe the promotion of unproven or fraudulent medical practices.*
- *The practice of fraudulent medicine, usually in order to make money or for ego gratification and power; health fraud; an instance of practicing fraudulent medicine*

Throughout the state of North Carolina—with no reason to think that Greensboro was an exception—considerable superstition was associated with medicine, as the vogue of faith healers testifies. One author declared in 1903:

> *It is a fact not now generally known that some of the early settlers regarded many diseases as directly due to the power and influence of witches…The methods of the so-called "witch doctors" were often ludicrous…There are traditional instances which relate how the "witch doctors" tried to cure cases of serious sickness…by reconciling any family differences with neighbors, even to the extent of returning all borrowed property, after which the treatment consisted of "words" or "prayers," sometimes accompanied with anointing the parts of the body which seemed to be the seat of the "witches" with concoctions, the making and compounding of which was a secret to all except those initiated.*

These quacks were of various sorts. A great many were mere vendors of nostrums, some of their own brewing and others of the patent medicine variety. They made no pretense at settling in a neighborhood and building up a practice but instead traveled from place to place on horseback or in their little carts selling their medicines as they went.

Dr. S.S. Satchwell recognized this problem in 1857 and issued the following declaration:

> *Thousands upon thousands, in our own State are daily denouncing medical science, and at the same time administering to themselves and families, the most powerful remedies in the shape of nostrums. They refuse the "mineral medicines," as they call them, of regular physicians, but are ready to follow the prescriptions of corrosive sublimate and*

> *arsenic, of itinerant wart and cancer doctors…A neighbor of mine, who is an honest, clever man, but noted for his want to confidence in physicians, recently paid a traveling quack one hundred dollars for a vial of drops, and the application of some mysterious mesmeric passes to one of his children, for the cure of epilepsy.*

Another type of quack was the one who professed to be able to cure ailments of a particular sort, such as cancer, carbuncles, polyps, warts or a particular disease, such as hydrophobia. A cancer doctor advertised in 1811 that he would sell his knowledge "on reasonable terms" as he had "some prospect of moving out of the State."

In 1852, Dr. Walter A. Norwood complained to the North Carolina Medical Society that "the people of the State seem to have agreed that any man who calls himself a Doctor, and owns a horse and a pair of medical saddlebags, shall be respected accordingly." Thus began a study of the various quacks "practicing" in North Carolina—Greensboro being no exception.

There were others who were considered quacks. Some swore they could cure "Cancer Worts; also Polypusses, or a Thing of that Nature." Another quack professed, "All diseases are the effect of one general cause and can be removed by one general remedy." His fee? "$20 to anyone wishing to practice on his family and for $100 to anyone wishing to practice on others." Still other antebellum quacks recommended hydropathy (or hydrotherapy, as we know it today), which included "the sponge bath, the wet-sheet packing, the sitz, foot and arm baths, the douche, the stream bath, the dripping sheet, the plunge, and the dry-blanket packing."

In December 1799, a group of doctors met and organized the North Carolina Medical Society. In 1820, North Carolina's Governor Branch "called attention to the adventurous Quack, presuming upon the ignorance and credulity of the people, and the Legislature responded with a bill to create a medical examining board." From 1827 to 1830, bills were introduced to regulate the practice of medicine. Not everyone agreed with regulating the practice of medicine through laws. "Quackery cannot be put down by legislation," these opponents declared. "If the people will be deceived, they will be deceived."

Smallpox Ordinance

NOTICE—Greensboro N.C., Dec. 29, 1860

Be it O'rdained by the Board of Commissioners of the Town of Greensborough, That all persons from the city of Columbia, S.C., or from any other place in the State, or any adjoining State, infected with Small Pox, are prohibited from coming into the town of Greensboro', under a penalty of $50, to be collected from any person in such case offending. And if any person from any place so infected, and not being informed of this ordinance, shall come into the town of Greensboro', he shall be required to depart immediately, under penalty of $10 for every hour he shall stay after being informed.

This Ordinance to lie in force until the danger of such infection shall subside.

Housekeeping Duties: Necessary Yet Demoralizing

Early publications like *The Carolina Housewife* or *The Lady's Token* instructed housewives on their duties. Details and rules abounded for cleaning, doing laundry, making soap and supervising the poultry yard and garden, according to Mrs. Mary Mason, who wrote on the specific duties of wife and mother:

A mistress must inspect every apartment daily to see that "the whole is swept, dusted, aired, and divested of cobwebs." Bedrooms should be aired daily and beds sunned twice a month. All kitchen utensils should be taken out doors once a week and scrubbed. Chimneys should be swept down every day in the winter before the fires were made and burned out once a month on a rainy day. Closet, cupboard, and pantry doors should be kept shut and locked to keep out cats, mice, and rats, and the mistress herself should carry the keys. If possible, she should strain the milk herself and see that the churns were scalded and aired daily. She should be on hand once or twice a month when the clothes were being sorted in the laundry, when starch was being made, and when bluing was being added to the rinsing water, for "servants have little idea of proportion" and quickly become careless. The mistress should grease the flat irons and later attend to the airing of the ironed clothes.

Mrs. Mason continued her explicit dictates by describing more wifely/motherly chores:

The mistress should begin housecleaning in February, "as vermin begin to lose their torpor about this time, and bestir themselves to prepare for a progeny." On some bright day, have all your beds moved out into the sun, shaken, dusted, and searched well. While the beds are sunning, search over all your bedsteads. Wipe them over with cold soapsuds, and carefully stop every crack, seam, and screw-hold with hard turpentine soap.

General housecleaning did not begin until the first of May, when the prudent housewife removed all furniture from the house, took up carpets, whitewashed all walls and ceilings, washed windows, and scrubbed all the woodwork. A bushel of unslacked lime, slacked in a barrel with boiling water and then whitened with a gallon of flour-paste and a little bluing, was sufficient to whitewash an entire house.

According to historical reports, one father wrote this letter to his daughter in 1846, after he had taken charge of his household a few days because of his wife's illness:

If it is not managed with great ability, sobriety, & good sense, the duty of house-keeping is dirty, demoralizing & debasing in a high degree… It confines one to a series of low pursuits, a course of filthy drudgery, & disgusting slovenliness, that have but little time for study or quiet meditation, & very little for improving conversation or refined society; & it is altogether unsuited to moral & religious enjoyment. It keeps one in perpetual agitation, anxiety, & apprehension; & has no pleasure equal to the pains, the toil, the privations & the suffering, which it is almost sure to impose.

Remedy for That Wicked Common Cold

In 1890, Lunsford Richardson, a pharmacist, came to Greensboro, which offered a great business opportunity for Richardson's desire to develop the perfect remedy for the common cold. A later newspaper account elaborates:

> *Almost immediately after settling in Greensboro, the three small Richardson children caught bad colds...Following the best practice of the time, the Richardsons treated their children with poultices, which were disagreeable to make and to use, and also with a vapor lamp, which required that all the windows in the room be tightly closed. The children did recover from their colds, but their father was highly dissatisfied with the methods of treatment for their illnesses.*
>
> *He began experimenting with an idea he had developed—a vaporizing salve that combined the best features of both the poultice treatment and the head-clearing vaporizer. He spent long hours...and finally perfected an ointment which is today known the world over as Vicks VapoRub.*

By 1930, VapoRub was known internationally and sales were high. Then came Vics Va-tro-nol, Vicks Medicated Cough Drops, Vicks Inhalers and Vicks Medicating Cough Syrup.

Bog and Mire

When the first automobiles appeared in Greensboro, citizens became aware of the condition of the city streets. Beneath them lay swamps and streams. According to one local historian, "The automobile is no respecter of springs, health giving or otherwise, when they interfere with travel." Town commissioners began bringing their streets in good order about 1829; they used this method:

> *When the streets are sideling, to place logs of wood on the lowest sides, to dig down the highest side and dig a ditch along the highest side so that the streets will be made level. They had worried along for 100 years,*

> *not knowing what to do about mud in rainy seasons and dust in dry times. The bog and mire especially presented a real problem—mud holes in Elm Street so deep that a horse would scarcely have filled them. In 1891, the* Patriot *warned that within the corporate limits "mud is so deep that to cross some of the streets is rendered dangerous to short legged men and children."*

RAMPANT POLIOMYELITIS SWEEPS GREENSBORO

The tragic epidemic of poliomyelitis hit Greensboro in 1947. A temporary treatment frame shack at the old World War II Overseas Replacement Depot (ORD) in northeast Greensboro housed the polio victims. By spring of 1948, new quarters replaced the first rustic makeshift hospital. Norris Hadaway, chairman of the Guilford County Chapter of the National Foundation for Infantile Paralysis, and city council's Mayor Fielding L. Fry made hasty arrangements to move the polio hospital to the North Greene Street former offices of the North Carolina Employment Service. Immediate care was available to over sixty patients.

Facilities were needed, however, for the new patients brought in by ambulance from sixteen other counties. By July 1948, the hospital had added forty-three new cases. A new facility was desperately needed; a hospital must be built! The city took seriously the cry for help. The *Greensboro Daily News* and the *Greensboro Record*, along with all the radio stations, urged citizens throughout North Carolina "to open both hearts and pocketbooks with the result that never before had so much money rolled into Greensboro for a universal cause." The call for help brought miraculous results:

> *The proposed temporary building was to cost $60,000. By the end of 14 days, an unofficial total of $100,000 had been contributed. The original idea of temporary buildings was discarded, and plans were redrawn for a permanent 125-bed modern hospital, unsurpassed in the state. A new goal of $175,000 was set, and with 42 days the total contributions passed $200,000 for the Central Carolina Convalescent Hospital.*

> *In addition to monetary contributions, volunteer workmen came from as far away as New York. Union and non-union laborers worked side by side to contribute over 11,000 man-hours of skilled and unskilled labor. Greensboro women prepared and served meals. After only 94 days "the shining palace that rose directly out of a cane field, opened to accept the scores that awaited." Twenty-three local doctors, representing every specialty and 160 hospital staff members cared for the patients.*

According to one historical account, when the hospital opened in 1948, an unidentified, gray-haired old man spat his tobacco juice and said, "Yep, it seems that it ain't rightly just a building at all…It's more like a kind of monument…A buildin's got to belong to somebody. That there building don't belong to nobody, and at the same time it belongs to everybody. If you started to take it apart and give a piece of it to everybody that owns a piece there just wouldn't be enough to go around!"

Interestingly, the horrible scourge of polio brought something new and progressive to Greensboro as "victims of poliomyelitis confined to the Central Carolina Convalescent Hospital had their non-segregated school which was fully supported by the city school system."

In Times of War

When World War II was declared, President Roosevelt said, "All of us are in it, every man, every woman, every child," and Greensboro "went to war." Textile mills made cloth for war services. The Vick Chemical plant produced "certain chemicals never before produced in this country." Citizens planted victory gardens. Women became welders, civilian pilot trainers, meter readers and machine workers. According to historian Ethel Arnett, wickedness again reared its head in the midst of goodness:

> *Two problems which appeared in Greensboro as well as in other localities were those of absenteeism and venereal disease. War production plants had difficulty in fulfilling their contracts because so many employees were absent from work.*

> *Greensboro leaders quickly recognized the seriousness of this prevalence of venereal disease as it reached alarming proportions during the early war period. Consequently, efforts for its control were drastically enforced, so that soon Greensboro had the lowest record of any camp site in the country. Greensboro was the site of an army camp, the only city in the United States to have an army camp of over 30,000 within its corporate limits. It turned out to be the Overseas Replacement Depot, commonly known as ORD, one of 3 in the country. Its presence quickly changed conditions in the city. With the great number of soldiers added to Greensboro's population, all "Blue Sunday" laws were lifted and motion pictures, bowling alleys, and all kinds of sports except pool halls were opened to the public.*

SEGREGATION-ERA LITERACY TEST

In the 1950s, Supreme Court Chief Justice Henry Frye, from Greensboro, was determined to persuade the other 119 legislators in the State House to abolish the segregation-era literacy test, which "had been used to keep blacks away from the voting booth." Frye worked diligently to assure that the bill would pass; he "made a list of the legislators with columns denoting *yes*, *no*, and *undecided.* Then he launched all-out support for the bill." Fellow legislators told him he was wasting his time. "You won't get that through the House or the Senate," they informed him. Frye said years later, "Frankly, I had some doubts myself." The bill passed after Frye shared with legislators this personal experience:

> *In 1956, Frye had spent the past six months in New York and had come home to marry his college sweetheart, Shirley Taylor. The 23-year-old spent the night before the wedding at his parents' home in Ellerbe, and decided to register to vote before heading to Greensboro. What he should have been asked to do, as part of an established literacy test, was read and write a section of the Constitution to the satisfaction of the registrar.*

> *"The guy started asking me all kinds of questions I knew were not a part of the literacy test, so I refused to try to answer the questions. 'Name the 14th president,' 'Name three signers of the Declaration of Independence.' Unnecessary questions. This was what black people had to deal with," Frye said. "I didn't forget about it.*

According to Frye, the passing of the bill "strengthened my belief in democracy."

PART III
Crimes and Punishments

Dungeons and Isolation

In 1848, when Dorothea Dix traveled across the state collecting information concerning the treatment of the insane, jail conditions had greatly improved. She reported a majority of the thirty-five county jails that she saw to be in good order. While she found only a few to be in excellent condition, she found only thirteen to be very defective, either from the poor construction of the building itself or from the lack of cleanliness in the "dungeons." She found, in many instances, that the jailor, "as should always be arranged," resided "in one part of the building, having thereby the more immediate and efficient care of the prison." The Guilford jail, located in Greensboro, was "isolated, but very well built and well kept: in addition to the dungeons and other strong rooms, was the unusual provision of a large chapel room for religious services." Dorothea Dix, however, found that "the Guilford County poorhouse, utterly comfortless and out of repair," was being abandoned for a $4,000 brick structure.

INCARNATION FOR THE WICKED

In the mid-1800s, the *Greensborough Patriot* supported building a new $100,000 state penitentiary where criminals would be punished.

> *The offense most frequently committed from the opening of the century to the close of the period in 1860 was that of disturbing the public peace. To this class belong such misdemeanors as assault and battery, affray, riot, rout, and unlawful assembly. The next most frequent offense was that against public morality and decency. Fornication and adultery and bastardy were the offenses of this order most frequently committed. Bastardy cases seldom came up for trial. Usually the reputed father came into court, admitted the charge, and gave bond for the support of the child according to law. The third offense most frequently committed in ante-bellum NC was that of being a public nuisance. Those most likely to be indicted in this manner were habitual drunkards, gamblers, prostitutes, common scolds, and petty trouble-makers, although a person committing annoyances in public roads, rivers, and bridges by actual obstruction or the neglect of repairs, and a person establishing a manufacture in such a place as to render the enjoyment of life and property uncomfortable were also liable to indictment as a common nuisance. The fourth most frequent offense was that of petit larceny, theft of an article under the value of 12 pence; the next, that of trespass; and after this, a host of misdemeanors punishable by fine.*

The *Greensborough Patriot* invited gentlemen to contribute essays on the subject of establishing a penitentiary to be owned and operated by the state for the reformation of the criminal class. In 1800, a bill was defeated in the House after days of debate. Finally, the legislature of 1844–45 took the first decisive step of the period toward the erection of a penitentiary. More with an eye to their own future in politics than to the interest of reform, the legislators refused to assume the responsibility for establishing the system and passed the question on to a popular vote to be held in August 1846 at the regular election for members of the legislature. The proposition as submitted to the people through the columns of the press called for a penitentiary costing $100,000. When the question at last came to a vote in August, it was overwhelmingly defeated.

Consequently, "some crimes passed totally unpunished, some property remained wholly unprotected, some laws continued in the statute book, to which obedience was never to be enforced. The murder of slaves and horse stealing seldom received the punishment prescribed by law."

School Apparatus: Multipurposed for Work and Punishment

According to historians, the early Greensboro teacher had three pieces of apparatus with which to conduct his school: a switch, a ferule and a pocketknife. We all know what the switch symbolized. The ferule served a double purpose, the flat side for inflicting blows upon the palm of the hand and the straight edge for marking lines upon unruled copy books. The knife was for cutting pens from goose quills.

Hangings: Public Celebrations

A hanging was attended with almost as much ceremony as a public celebration and attracted even greater crowds:

> *The gallows was a simple, though effective, arrangement. A beam was placed between two trees; and after the adjustment of the rope, the cart on which the prisoner was standing was driven from under the beam. The spectacle of the victim struggling to keep his feet on the moving cart filled the crowd with a kind of delightful horror so that a different mode of execution was finally devised. The rap which thus came into use was held up by a rope which was passed over a beam and cut at the desired moment. The prisoner, seated on his coffin, was driven in a cart to the place of execution. He often was shrouded in a robe and accompanied to the gallows by ministers, likewise shrouded and very grave. Sometimes the prisoner exhorted the spectators and nearly always he spoke a few last words. Instances are on record in*

> *which the prisoner was first conducted to church where a sermon was preached before a large audience which later accompanied the culprit to the gallows.*

On the day of a public hanging, the village was usually crowded with eager spectators. Men, women and children came in their best attire and made a holiday of the occasion.

SLAVES: ARRESTS AND PUNISHMENT FOR RUNAWAYS

Old records in the Greensboro Public Library throw some light on the local slavery situation. The minute book of the organized town of Greensboro in 1829 showed that there were then 18 free Negroes, 102 slaves and 33 families who owned slaves. One man, Robert Carson, had 15, and the next highest number owned was 6. The average was 2 or 3.

According to the town rules, the free Negroes and the whites were treated alike in case of correction—that is, to appear before the town officials and give an account of themselves. The law governing slaves was more rigid: "It shall be the duty of the Patrol to arrest all slaves whoever they may find on the streets, kitchens, where they do not belong (except such Negroes as have wives and not to be interrupted at their wives) or else when off their overseers or hirers lots after ten o'clock at night, the Patrol may whip the slaves by them taken up not exceeding fifteen lashes."

The *Greensborough Patriot* in 1826 printed a notice of a runaway slave, with a five-cent reward offered by Mitchell Wood for his return. In 1829, the *Patriot* printed this notice:

> *RUN AWAY BOY*
> *TEN CENTS REWARD*
> *The above reward will be given to any person who will return said boy to the subscriber but no expense will be paid or thanks given—Asa Hunt*

Dates and Events: Association with Local Murder Trial

The weekly periodical the *Greensborough Patriot* debuted with the April 24, 1826 issue. The publisher of this weekly was T. Early Strange. In the first issue, Strange announced that he had purchased an earlier paper, the *Carolina Patriot.* There is some uncertainly about the *Carolina Patriot*'s beginning date. It is said to have been published in the year 1821, and there is some evidence to bear out that statement:

> *Joseph Reece, first editor of* The Daily Record, *wrote that he once encountered a very old farmer who peddled eggs in Greensboro. "See here," said the old man, "the* [founding] *date on that* Patriot *is wrong. It's 1821 and I'll tell you how I come to know. In the year 1821 there was a big murder case on trial at the courthouse here and I had come up to hear it. I was standing on the corner where the* Patriot *office is when along come one of them journey-man printers. He was drunk…and when he got to the corner he fell sprawling into a page of the* Patriot *type put out in the sun to dry. And that's why I know the* Patriot *was published that year." Reece looked up the date of the mentioned murder case and found it was in the year 1821.*

Prostitution

In 1822, concerned commissioners started a campaign against prostitution, and that same year, the legislature investigated different ways to make laws more strict in this way: "Three persons of good character could charge another of ill fame before a justice of peace. If the charge was proved, the offender was subject to an imprisonment of ten days and after that she was to be hired out to the highest bidder for a term sufficient to pay all costs. The persons giving the information were to receive 'ten dollars in compensation.'"

According to one North Carolina historian, prostitutes attended fairs, musters and courtrooms: "Scores of women attend court for the sole purpose of drinking and pandering to the lustful passions of dirty men,

Street walkers.

The whore's last shift.

and I regret so exceedingly to say, that some men, I will not say gentlemen, are guilty of intercourse with these dirty, filthy strumpets, that ought to be, and one would think they are above doing such things."

Punishments for Wickedness

At the beginning of the nineteenth century, the State of North Carolina prescribed the punishment of death without benefit of clergy in at least twenty-eight instances:

> *Arson, burglary, murder, highway robbery, accessories before the fact in each of these four crimes—treason, housebreaking in the day time and taking off goods to the amount of 20 shillings, bestiality or sodomy, dueling, bigamy, stealing slaves or aiding them to escape, stealing free Negroes from the State and selling them, voluntary return of slaves*

transported from the State by sentence of court, rebellion of slaves or conspiracy to incite insurrection, free persons joining a conspiracy or rebellion of slaves, concealing childbirth, breach of prison by a person committed for a felony, counterfeiting notes of the Bank of North America, and the second offenses of manslaughter, forgery, horse-stealing, maiming by putting out eyes or disabling the tongue, counterfeiting or knowingly passing counterfeited bills of credit, public certificates, or lottery tickets; robbery except in a dwelling house or near a highway; larceny from the person to an amount of 12 pence or upwards; too great duress of imprisonment on the part of a jailor; embezzling or vacating records in a court of judicature; and embezzlement by a servant more than eighteen years old of his master's goods to the value of $10 or upwards.

Dismemberment "was the punishment next more severe to that of death as prescribed by the penal code in effect in North Carolina in 1817." The crimes that warranted this punishment were as follows:

First offense of maiming as to eye or tongue, perjury, subordination of perjury, the first offense of counterfeiting or constructing instruments for counterfeiting the bills of credit of 1783 or any public certificates, and the first offense of passing or attempting to pass knowingly such bills or certificates. The punishment, as in the case of perjury, was the loss of both ears and an additional punishment of a fine, not exceeding 500 pounds, standing in the pillory for one hour, and a disqualification to give testimony thereafter; in the case of malicious maiming, the loss of both ears, standing in the pillory two hours, and the infliction of thirty-nine lashes on the bare back.

ARCHIBALD DEBOW MURPHEY'S IMPRISONMENT

According to historical sources, Archibald Debow Murphey "was in chronic financial distress, having turned a comfortable financial position in 1812 into financial shambles by 1820. He was regularly overextended and unable to pay his debts. In 1829, he was imprisoned in Greensboro for 20 days because he could not pay a note when it became due."

It seems that Murphey, active in business, legal and political affairs, was an 1817 advocate of a publicly financed system of education and an 1819 recommendation for internal improvements for roads, rivers and canals. According to one historian, "Murphey's vision of the future surpassed that of his generation. He gave up his position as superior court judge after only two years because of his deteriorating financial condition."

Lyndon Swaim's article in an 1883 issue of the *Greensboro Patriot* recalls Murphey's Greensboro imprisonment:

> *His honor was unspotted. He was the victim of a law inflicting torture as exquisite to the sensitive soul, if not to the body, as the rack or thumb screw of the Middle Ages. I heard good old Sheriff Doak say that no occurrence of his life, official or otherwise, was so painful to him as the* [sentence] *upon the venerable judge, the meekness and dignity of whose bearing was so impressive, and his resignation to the inevitable so touching. When he was conducted to the prison and surveyed the surroundings…he remarked that the room was not…sufficiently lighted or ventilated. He requested the sheriff to leave the door open! And the sheriff went off and left the door open!*

Historical reports indicate that Judge Murphey never tried to leave the jail. It seems that when a friend and colleague, Judge Camero, confronted the sheriff about leaving the jail door unlocked, the sheriff replied, "I would risk life and sacred honor with Judge Murphey. You don't think he would go away?"

Judge Camero countered, "I do not mean that. I mean that it might be considered in law an escape, and you might yourself become involved to your hurt." The sheriff replied, "Murphey knows the law, let us go back and consult him." And when they did, Judge Murphey responded with these words: "Mr. Sheriff, my friend, it will be safest for you to lock the door upon me."

HANDCUFFED AND CHAINED

Born in 1798 near Greensboro, North Carolina, Levi Coffin grew up working on the family farm. He was still a youngster when he experienced this wickedness of slave owners:

> *In the early 1800s, he came face-to-face with the institution of slavery. One day while he was out with his father chopping wood by the side of a road, a group of slaves, handcuffed and chained together, passed by on their way to be sold in Georgia, Alabama, and Louisiana. Questioned by the young boy's father about why they were chained, one of the men sadly replied: "They have taken us away from our wives and children, and they chain us lest we should make our escape and go back to them." After the dejected company had left the scene, the youth wondered to himself how he would feel if his father were taken away from him.*

In his later memoirs, Levi Coffin acknowledged this incident being the beginning for his "strong hatred of oppression and injustice in any form…and were the motives that influenced my whole after-life." While still a young man in his teens, he found this opportunity to assist a slave:

> *Attending a corn husking, the fifteen-year-old Coffin noticed a group of slaves brought to the husking by a slave dealer named Stephen Holland. While the other whites in the party dined, the Quaker boy remained behind to talk with the slaves and to "see if I could render them any service." He learned that one of the slaves, named Stephen, was freeborn and a former indentured servant to Edward Lloyd, a Philadelphia Quaker, but later had been kidnapped and sold into slavery. Thinking fast, Coffin arranged with a "trusty negro, whom I knew well," to take Stephen the next night to his father's house. After learning the particular of the now slave's case, the elder Coffin wrote Lloyd of his former servant's plight and eventually Stephen was liberated from slavery.*

In New Garden, then a part of Greensboro, Levi and his cousin Vestal Coffin supervised a Sunday school for blacks. Slaves were taught to read in a new and different way: with the Bible. As might be expected, slave owners, afraid of what their slaves might do if they were educated, forced the closing of the classes.

Levi Coffin left the Greensboro area about 1826, moving first to Indiana and later to Virginia and Paris, France. However, he never forgot his experiences as a young man, and he eventually earned the title "President of the Underground Railroad" because he befriended fugitives "who came to the Coffin's home at all hours of the night and announced their presence by a gentle rap at the door":

> *"I would invite them, in a low tone," said Coffin, "to come in, and they would follow me into the darkened house without a word, for we knew not who might be watching and listening." Once safely inside, the slaves would be fed and made comfortable for the evening. The number of fugitives varied considerably through the years, Coffin noted, but annually averaged more than one hundred.*

Swigging, Gambling and Swearing

During the later part of the eighteenth century, ministers in Greensboro became extremely concerned about the prevalence of gambling, heavy drinking, card playing, reveling, swearing and cursing. Revival meetings, offering spiritual "refreshing," were common occurrences and usually concluded with manifestation of spiritual blessings. At one service, according to William Paisley of Cross Roads Church, when no obvious blessings had come to the congregation, one parishioner stood up and said in a calm but earnest voice, "Stand still and see the salvation of God!" This is what happened next:

> *In five minutes, more or less, scores were crying for mercy. Many were struck down, or thrown in to a state of helplessness if not of insensibility… Bating* [sic] *the miraculous attestations from Heaven, such as cloven tongues like fire and the power of speaking different languages, it was like a day of Pentacost and none was careless or indifferent…so deeply were the people absorbed…that they could not be got away from the place until the shades of evening had closed around them.*

The drunkards' pilgrimage.

Punishment for gamblers.

Obviously, these types of annual camp meeting revivals powerfully affected many who attended and showed many their sinful and wicked ways.

Not everyone, however, was religiously moved. On the contrary, there was scoffing, ridicule and open defiance of the meetings by some. There were liquor peddling, drunkenness and other abuses. And there were those who chose to look upon the camp gatherings as a sort of entertainment—"tares among the wheat." But despite these disadvantages, these revivals continued almost to the outbreak of the Civil War.

O. Henry (William Sydney Porter)

At the age of nineteen, Greensboro's "Master of the Short Story" became a licensed pharmacist in his uncle's Greensboro drugstore. One year later, he moved to Austin, Texas, where he lived on a ranch and continued working as a pharmacist. After four years of this work, he took a teller's job at the First National Bank in Austin. That's where his troubles began:

> *In 1894, Austin's First National Bank discovered it was missing money, dating back to the time Porter had worked. He was accused of embezzlement, though historians have speculated that the missing funds were probably due to bad bookkeeping rather than outright theft. Nevertheless, Porter skipped his train from Houston to Austin and went to New Orleans instead, fleeing his trial and leaving his wife and children behind. From New Orleans, he trekked to Honduras and South America, where he spent two years. Historical rumor suggests he was on the lamb with notorious South American criminals, using their $30,000 robbery booty to fund the trips. In 1897, however, Porter learned that his wife was seriously ill, and he returned to the United States to care for her. She died soon after, and he finally faced the criminal trial he had run from. Porter was tried on an embezzlement charge, and sentenced to five years in the Ohio State Penitentiary.*

Historians report that O. Henry's writing career lasted under ten years, but during this time he published ten collections of short stories. He died alcoholic and poor on June 5, 1910.

DRUG LORD FRANK LUCAS

Frank Lucas, born in 1930, was reared in Greensboro. According to one historian, Lucas "claims that the incident that sparked his motivation to embark on a life of crime was witnessing his 12-year-old cousin's murder at the hands of the Ku Klux Klan, for apparently 'reckless eyeballing (looking at a Caucasian woman).'"

And what a life of crime resulted from that Greensboro tragedy. Lucas's mother encouraged him to flee to New York, where he worked for gangster Bumpy Johnson and then moved on to Thailand, where he met up with one of his cousin's husband, Ike Atkinson. "Ike knew everyone over there, every black guy in the Army, from the cooks on up," Lucas admitted in a *New York Magazine* interview, explaining the way they smuggled drugs:

> *We did it, all right…ha, ha, ha…Who is hell is gonna look in a dead soldier's coffin? Ha he ha…We had him make up 28 copies of the government coffins…except we fixed them up with false bottoms, big enough to load up with six, maybe eight kilos…It had to be snug. You couldn't have shit sliding around. Ike was very smart, because he made sure we used heavy guys' coffins. He didn't put them in no skinny guys.*

Ironically, the place that sparked Lucas's life of crime was the same place that held many of his connections, as reported in one historical article:

> *Lucas only trusted relatives and close friends from North Carolina to handle his various heroin operations. Lucas thought they were less likely to steal from him and be tempted by various vices in the big city. He stated his heroin, "Blue Magic," was 98–100% pure when shipped from Thailand. Lucas has been quoted as saying that his worth was "something like $52 million," most of it in Cayman Islands banks.*

In 1976, Frank Lucas was sentenced to 70 years in prison, but he was released in 1981 upon serving 5 years. Convicted again in 1984, he was released in 1991 after serving a term of 7 years.

His career was dramatized in the 2007 feature film *American Gangster*, in which Frank Lucas is played by Denzel Washington.

Different Rules

In 1966, six years after the Greensboro Four sit-ins, some lunch counters still did not serve blacks. One such restaurant, the Apple Cellar, located near the University of North Carolina at Greensboro (UNCG), refused service to African Americans. Nelson Johnson, a student enrolled in North Carolina Agricultural and Technical State University, one of Greensboro's black colleges, was among the protesters. According to author Elizabeth Wheaton, this is what transpired:

Police arrested the white students for "violating dress codes" and took them from the restaurant. When the blacks went outside to protest the arrests, they were charged with interfering with a police officer and hauled off to jail. A judge later dismissed the charges against the white students. Johnson and the other black students were convicted.

Integrated groups, including Johnson, again invaded the Apple Cellar. This time a police officer told them that if they did not leave immediately there would be "trouble." The students took the hint. When they emerged from the Cellar, however, the trouble was already there and waiting: a line of about thirty men in blue uniforms and silver helmets shouting racial epithets. It was the Klan…

The students were forced to walk—slowly and quietly—past their tormentors to get to their cars. Humiliated, frustrated, angry, Johnson began to recognize the futility of working within a system of which blacks were not, and maybe never could be, a part—the futility of playing by the rules when the rules themselves were different for blacks and whites.

Johnson went on to form the Greensboro Association of Poor People (GAPP), composed of students from A&T, Bennett College and Dudley High School. His goal, according to Elizabeth Wheaton, was as follows:

> *His dream of a campus-community coalition was becoming a reality—and a threat, or so the city powers thought, based on reports funneled through the FBI to city police from a GAPP informant. Apparently no one in law enforcement bothered to double-check when the informant said that GAPP was a Black Panther front. It was not. No one bothered to double-check when the informant said that the group advocated violence and was arming itself. It was not.*
>
> *So, in the spring of 1969, when GAPP member Claude Barnes was elected student body president at Dudley on a write-in ballot, city officials pressed the school to void his election. The school capitulated, installing Barnes's runner-up. Over the next few weeks, the tension at Dudley and A&T rose in direct proportion to the heavy-handedness of school and city authorities. Some students were expelled; others walked out in protest. More students were expelled; more walked out. They sought help from their friends at A&T, and the campus seethed.*
>
> *Again, the city called for the National Guard and imposed a curfew. And again, gunfire erupted. This time an A&T student, Willie Grimes, was killed.*

Nelson Johnson then withdrew from the Greensboro Association of Poor People and formed the Student Organization for Black Unity (SOBU), bringing together students from A&T, Bennett and Malcolm X Liberation University, recently moved from Durham to Greensboro.

PROTESTOR, VIOLATOR OF ZONING LAWS AND BOMB THREAT

E.H. Hennis of Greensboro became a nemesis of county commissioners and took his protests too far, according to reporter David Nivens, who describes Hennis in this way: "At public meetings, he's the elderly man who brings protest posters and wears T-shirts with slogans critical of county officials he disdains." Supposedly, these actions are considered fairly harmless in light of Hennis's other protests:

> *When he held up what appeared to be a bomb at a commissioners meeting, threatening to blow county officials to bits, the next gavel he would hear would be in a criminal courtroom. "I am angry, but I do have fun with it," Hennis has said to news reporters through the years. In 1993, after six Democratic commissioners voted for a property-tax increase, Hennis hung all six in effigy from a billboard outside his home. Most of Hennis' tirades refer to a bitter land-use battle he fought with the county in the late 1990s after a judge ordered him to clear more than 20 abandoned mobile homes from his property.*
>
> *Hennis refused, so Guilford County intervened by hauling 91 truckloads of salvage—mobile homes, equipment and debris—from his property. Hennis sued for $300,000 and proclaimed to leaders, "Your body parts will be picked up and put in body bags" as he held up what appeared to be a pipe bomb.*

According to Nivens, Hennis is known as "a retired demolitions expert and former Ku Klux Klan leader":

> *Much of the folklore surrounding Hennis goes back to the Klan's activities in the 1960s and 1970s. In 1969 Hennis, then reputed to be a former exalted Cyclops, protested in front of the Guilford County Courthouse in Greensboro with a sandwich-board sign that read "Impeach Judge Allen Gwyn" and "Unfair to white people." During the November 3, 1979, shootout between Klansmen and members of the Communist Workers Party at Morningside Homes in Greensboro, Hennis was a city police informant, Hennis told* YES! Weekly *in a 2007 interview. Greensboro's Truth and Reconciliation Commission did not use Hennis' comments in the final commission report, however, because researchers were unable to confirm his claim that police officers were active in the Klan.*

A judge eventually barred Hennis from filing more lawsuits without permission from a court.

PART IV
The Cutting Edge

Shooting Matches and Cock Fighting

One of the most interesting events in the colonial history of recreation in Guilford County might never have taken place if the legislature had not passed a law to increase agriculture harvests. This law required that each man in the region kill five crows, fifty blackbirds and five squirrels per year or pay a fine. The men of Greensboro obeyed the law. Each killed his quota of these creatures, which were destructive to crops, and all the people made a celebration of the slaughtering by holding a shooting match. At a designated meeting place, the shooters would turn over their kill to the sheriff. Then, with the women proudly watching, the men would demonstrate their marksmanship. The clumsy old flintlock rifle performed with pinpoint precision in the hands of a pioneer.

Addison Coffin in his *Early Settlements of Friends in North Carolina* records this story:

> *There was a shooting match about one mile east of where Guilford College now stands, in a forest.* [A large company of noted riflemen were performing wonderful feats of marksmanship.] *In the midst of the exciting contest a beautiful young woman suddenly made her appearance coming up the road from the northwest. She was dressed*

in a neat walking dress with ornamented Indian leggings and moccasins. She carried a small rifle highly ornamented with silver mountings, and the usual shot pouch and belt, with hunting knife and small hatchet, a complete hunting outfit. After the excitement had somewhat subsided and shooting began again, she modestly asked permission to take a shot with the contestants; the request was granted and she stepped lightly out of the line, raised her rifle, took quick aim and fired, the ball drove the center to a hair's breath sixty yards away. A shout of applause from the hunters made the forest ring. Again she loaded and fired, again the ball drove the center. Astonished and bewildered the old hunters gathered around her, doubting whether they were seeing a vision, or were in the presence of flesh and blood, but her bright intelligent face, respectful language, and lady-like bearing convinced them that she was a mortal, and one of the highest types of sacred womanhood, but to the inquiry who she was, from whence she came, and why thus alone among strangers, she respectfully declined to answer, but gave her name as Ann, the huntress. Richard Dodson, a Friend, invited her to go home with him…she accepted the invitation and as they walked away her form was so graceful and her step so light and springing that the old veterans shook their heads again doubting whether or not all was really human.

She stayed at the Dodson home and acted as family huntress and teacher for the children. In the winter of 1807–8 Ann disappeared as suddenly as she appeared and no trace of her was ever found.

A common sport was the challenge to remove with one shot both eyes of a turkey tied eighty yards away. This was called "gander pulling." Someone would suspend from the limb of a tree a tough old gander with its neck well saturated with grease and soft soap. Then mounted contestants, while riding at full speed, would try to pull the fowl's head off.

Horse racing and cock fighting are said to have been Andrew Jackson's favorite pastimes while he lived in Guilford. His old race paths are still pointed out around Summerfield. Whatever the play, it was not unusual to find betting, heavy drinking and even fighting at various meets.

The first property census of Greensboro, taken in 1829, recorded "five stores, three retail liquor stores, and a stud horse." All were located around what was known as Courthouse Square. The town at that time boasted 369 people, which, according to one historical report, "averaged a store for about every 74 people."

Robert Moderwell has been cited as "the town's most successful early merchant," and his merchandise was a conglomeration of goods:

> *This thriving store sold nails, sugar, molasses, iron, turpentine, glass, resin, putty, and lead, and school books. For the wares Moderwell accepted cash or produce. Acceptable barter included eggs, tallow, beeswax, honey, dried fruit, sorghum, corn, wheat, cured meat, furs, and other articles. Liquids were usually stored in barrels with faucets for letting out whatever the customers wanted. Whiskey was freely served with a dipper and passed to the customer in a tumbler, mug, or even sometimes in the dipper itself. Such a swigging is understandable in view of the fact that the town's water pumps were so often out of order!*

Sippin' and Dippin'

Prosperous farmers gave annual corn shuckings for their neighbors. The host would place upon a long table in the yard beef and mutton stews, roasted sweet potatoes, pumpkin pies and apples. Jugs of whiskey and brandy were plentiful and were patronized so frequently that many guests would fall asleep in the shucks. At midnight, when the crowd had dispersed, the thoughtful host would drag the drowsy ones into the house and lay them on the floor by the fire. Those whom too much whisky made quarrelsome would sometimes come to blows and break up the gathering with a brawl.

Quilting was a long and tedious task if done by one woman; but when the housewife was assisted by a dozen neighbors, she might complete the quilt in a day. For such a quilting bee, the guests would usually assemble in the morning, bringing their own needles and thimbles. Amid a lively conversation, needles would fly back and forth. Scattered over the surface of the quilt might be seen four or five round tin boxes containing pungent Scotch snuff. Now and then a seamstress would take from her mouth a small black stick from three to four inches in length and, after dipping it in the snuffbox, rub her teeth briskly with it. This process completed, she would resume her work, continually moving the brush up and down or from side to side, engaging in conversation all the while. Some dippers, less expert than others, would soon have their snuff, like an overseer's wages, spread "from y-ear to y-ear."

In 1833, Henry Barnard of Connecticut was surprised to find in North Carolina that "the ladies, are fine ladies, eat snuff," and if gentlemen come in "all the apparatus will disappear as if by magic." The country women, however, were open in their habit of snuff dipping and were not ashamed when they came to market to walk along the streets with brushes in their mouths. In 1845, a correspondent of the *Carolina Watchman* thought that the use of snuff was a family habit among all ranks of female society throughout the length and breadth of the state. A European gentleman once offered his snuffbox to a lady in North Carolina, and to his amazement, she thrust in a toothbrush. While he was waiting to see how she would poke it up her nose, he was even more amazed to see the brush disappear into the lady's mouth. In 1855, the *Carolina Cultivator* was still condemning the habit of "snuff rubbing" among the women of the state.

"Dance frolkicks" were popular community events. Mint-sling, blackberry acid and cider were served between dances, and not infrequently, the men also had their whiskey and brandy. But as the camp meeting movement grew more popular, dancing came to be frowned upon. The fiddle became an instrument of the devil, and the pious looked upon the mere possession of one as an indication of an irreligious spirit.

Most of the taverns were log huts or rough weather-boarded buildings. The more prosperous ones consisted of several rooms, but most of them had only one large room with no interior division. In one corner was the family bunk, in another a pine chest and in a third a railing that formed the bar. Upon this a rum keg and a rumbler were arrayed. Visitors could often recognize an ordinary, on emerging from the woods, "by an earthen jug suspended by the handle from a pole. The pipe of the chimney never rising above the roof; or a score of black hogs luxuriating in the sunshine and mud before the door."

Such was the country tavern of 1800 ordinaries, as they were sometimes called. Farmers met to talk politics, play at all fours (a card game similar

Barroom dancing.

to seven up and muggings; the players built in suits or matched exposed cards, the object being to get rid of the cards as quickly as possible), make bets and stand treat for mint-sling or brandy.

The bar was probably the chief attraction of the tavern, for drinking was common, and here could be obtained liquors that could not be made at home. The sale of West Indian and continental rum, claret, Madeira, port and Tenerife wine, besides the domestic whiskey, beer, wine and cider, formed an important part of tavern business. The tendency to run up large bills for liquor led to a law prohibiting a "keeper of an inn, tavern, or ordinary, or retailer of liquors by then small measure," from selling liquors on credit of a greater amount than ten dollars unless the person so credited should sign a note for the debt.

Habitual drunkenness was quite generally frowned upon, but no stigma was attached to "restrained drinking." In fact, a moderate use of liquor was generally considered healthful. Grog was often taken before breakfast to whet the appetite and "to keep the fevers off." Fretful babies were soothed with a teaspoonful of diluted liquor, reputed to be a certain cure for colic

No holiday was thought to have been celebrated properly unless one succeeded in "getting a little corned." The *Greensboro Patriot* editor, Lyndon Swaim, who promised that his "whole intellectual energies shall be exerted to render the contents of its columns both useful and interesting to every class in the community," published this humorous editorial about drinking:

> *Pyramid of Drink—the effects of drink in its various degrees was represented by a pyramid, thus:*
>
> *Tipsy*
> *
> *Very Fresh* * * *Very Tipsy*
> *Fresh* * * * *Drunk*
> *Lively* * * * * *Very Drunk*
> *Comfortable* * * * * * *Stupidly Drunk*
> *Sober* * * * * * * *Dead Drunk*

Of course, whiskey was also used for medicinal purposes. Traveling dentists in 1833 accommodated ladies and gentlemen by paying visits to their homes. The dentist offered spirits before the days of anesthetics. A good-sized drink of whiskey helped deaden the pain when a tooth had to be pulled. Dr. J.S. Betts recalled one pain-ridden patient who drank his "anesthetic" and then, feeling no pain while the dentist was preparing for the extraction, quietly slipped out of the office and was never seen again.

Irony abounded in Greensboro's turn-of-the-twentieth-century establishment of sanitariums. One was the Keeley Institute, established in 1891 by Judge W.H. Eller and associates. Located on the second floor of Central Hotel at the southwest corner of Courthouse Square, the institute had some wicked competition. Beneath the hotel and the alcoholic rehabilitation institute was, of all things, a saloon. But before the institute moved to its present location at Blandwood, the saloonkeeper came upstairs, took the treatment and moved to a farm in the country, where he ended his days as a teetotaler.

Surrogate Babysitter

Greensboro's first telephone appeared in Greensboro in 1880. George S. Sergeant, manufacturer and inventor of machinery, bought a pair of telephones for twenty-five dollars and installed them in his office and home, about one-third of a mile apart. According to one historian, "The queer contraption carried the human voice which spread like the wind for there were no ear pieces and all standing within the room could hear." A local newspaper gave the following humorous report:

The instrument replaced the nurse in the Sergeant household. If Mrs. Sergeant wished to go shopping, she would telephone: "George, I'm going up town; you take care of the children," and papa would. Through the telephone he would listen, and if the children started scrapping, his voice would fill the room with fatherly admonitions. Sergeant found the new instrument so useful that he bought two other pairs and connected them with Wakefield Hardware and Odell Hardware; and soon other businesses began to install the mechanical voice.

Potential Bank Raid Thwarted

The Bank of Cape Fear, established in Greensboro in 1851, was located in the first block of South Elm Street. Jesse Lindsay, cashier and ultimately leading financier, authorized John C. Wharton to take any necessary steps to prevent a potential bank raid. This it was happened, as noted by one historian:

Jesse Lindsay, fearing a federal raid during the Civil War, confided to John C. Wharton that in the bank's vault there were then $10,000 to $15,000 in gold and silver and that it must be hidden at once, the hiding place to be left to Wharton. Under the cover of night, therefore, Wharton came into the town on horseback and carried the bank specie to his farm, dug a hole in the woods, and buried the money. He then built a pig pen over the spot and placed a litter of pigs over the treasure. After the danger of confiscation had passed, the gold and silver were

Pigpen.

safely returned to the bank. Whether or not the bank remained open, its building was sold in 1869 to Julius Gray, and he with Jesse Lindsay and Eugene Morehead reorganized the remains of the Greensboro branch of the Bank of Cape Fear into the Bank of Greensboro.

"The Forgotten Man": For Women Only

Walter Hines Page, educated at Trinity College (Duke University), was on the staff of the *New York Evening Post*. In 1895, he became literary adviser to Houghton, Mifflin and Company and editor of the *Atlantic Monthly*. In June 1897, Page presented his famous speech entitled "The Forgotten Man" to female students at the North Carolina State Normal and Industrial School in Greensboro.

Page began his speech talking about the forgotten man and the lack of education for the masses because "the stationary social condition indicated by generations of illiteracy had long been the general condition.

State Normal School #1, Greensboro, North Carolina.

State Normal School #2, Greensboro, North Carolina.

The forgotten man was content to be forgotten. He became not only a dead weight, but a definite opponent of social progress."

Page's transition in his famous speech admits his real mission. He said, "I have thus far spoken only of the forgotten man. I have done so to show the social and educational structure in proper perspective." Following is an excerpt that denotes his real purpose:

> *But what I have come to speak about is the forgotten woman. Both the aristocratic and the ecclesiastical systems made provision for the women of special classes—the fortunately born and the religious well-to-do. But all the other women were forgotten. Let any man whose mind is not hardened by some worn-out theory of politics or of ecclesiasticism go to the country in almost any part of the State and make a study of life there, especially the life of the women. He will see them thin and wrinkled in youth from ill prepared food, clad without warmth or grace, living in untidy houses, working from daylight till bed-time at the dull round of weary duties, the slaves of men of equal slovenliness, the mothers of joy-less children—all uneducated if not illiterate.*

Page concluded his speech to the women of the State Normal and Industrial School by issuing this challenge: "The battle will be practically won when the whole State shall stand on this platform: A public school system generously supported by public sentiment, and generously maintained by both State and local taxation, is the only effective means to develop the forgotten man, and even more surely the only means to develop the forgotten woman."

EARLY AMBULANCE SERVICE

One of Greensboro's newspapers, the *Record*, described the town's first ambulance service:

> *Just when the afternoon was the hottest, carriages, passersby, drays, and* [bicycles] *gave way to an old surrey from which the high seats*

> *had been removed. On the "bed" where the benches had been, was a straw "pallet." A suffering invalid lay there, attended by a doctor or kinswoman who fanned at multitudinous flies while the driver wended his way carefully...*[In winter] *smothering blankets ill protected* [patients] *from cold and rain.*

One Greensboro citizen, Mrs. G.W. Whitsett, could not bear to witness the wickedness of transporting seriously ill people, so she and Mrs. T.J. Copeland organized Greensboro's first ambulance society "to purchase and maintain one or more ambulances for the transportation of persons who are ill or maimed from one place in the city to another."

First Tornado: Funnel-Shaped with Tip Glowing

The *Record* reported Greensboro's first tornado at twilight on Thursday evening, April 2, 1936, in this way: "Funnel-shaped, with tip glowing like fire in light reflected, it came swirling and rushing, dipping to earth here and there as it swept on an east, northeast course, leaving a trail of wreckage, fire, injury, and death in its wake. It was gone in the span of a few minutes—almost before anyone realized it was happening."

According to historical reports, "The tops of buildings were lifted off like bonnets, and walls were ripped apart and dismantled leaving the people inside victims to its fury. Within about two and a half minutes the tempest had left 12 dead, over 100 wounded, and property damaged estimated at $1,500.000."

The twister produced these other problems:

> *As soon as the twister had passed, fires flamed from wrecked factories and homes; screams of fire trucks, ambulances, police cars, and locomotives resounded; and wails and shrieks of victims pierced the air. And then, adding to the general alarm and confusion, the city was plunged in darkness, for Duke Power Company had found it necessary to cut off the current to prevent the outbreak of additional fires. The city was not left in darkness for long, however, for the skies quickly cleared, and the*

> *moon and stars came out. Within about 4 hours lights were on again in most sections of the city which had not been ravaged.*
>
> *Rescue workers, who went about their work, were hindered by thousands of Greensboro curiosity seekers who roamed the city's streets.*

The *Record* reported on April 3 the following update: "The picture presented this morning, as the rays of the sun broke over the horizon, was one of tragedy…untold suffering, people homeless, their earthly possessions taken from them in one burst of nature's fury." Rescue work continued to help Greensboro recover from its first tornado.

RED NOVEMBER, BLACK NOVEMBER

The premiere showing of the film *Red November, Black November* was held on March 1, 1981, at a theatre in the Greensboro Coliseum complex. Security consisted of Greensboro police offices and Communist Workers Party patrols. Over two hundred people had shown up for this event. Elizabeth Wheaton's account of that evening is a true story:

> *In the corridor, a reporter spotted a familiar face. She approached him cautiously. "How ya doin?"*
>
> *"Pretty good, pretty good. And yourself?"*
>
> *"Okay. Kinda risky coming out here tonight, isn't it?"*
>
> *"I just want to see what they're saying about me. It's open to the public, and I'm part of the public."*
>
> *Someone signaled that the film was about to start and the two walked to the ticket booth. "Two?" the reporter was asked.*
>
> *"No, no. We're not together." She paid for one ticket and walked quickly to the theater entrance. Tom Clark was taking tickets.*
>
> *"Who was that man you were talking to?" he asked.*
>
> *"Ed Dawson." She went inside and took a seat near the back, wondering what would happen next. The widow and families were all in the front row, oblivious to the gaunt, gray-haired man taking his seat at the end of a center row. Voices could be heard in the hallway outside. Moments later Sally Alvarez walked down the aisle. She stopped at*

Dawson's seat and looked straight into his eyes. "You are not welcome here, Mr. Dawson," she whispered. "Please leave quietly. We will return your money." Dawson did as he was told.

As the film began, the word spread quickly through the audience. Ed Dawson was here. Walked right past all the police, all the security. It was an outrage. The murmuring settled down after a few minutes. There were the videotapes, the horrible videotapes, and many in the audience were reliving their own personal horror of November 3. The narrator talked about Ed Dawson and Bernie Butkovich, the Greensboro police, the FBI, the ATF—and political assassination.

Historian Elizabeth Wheaton takes us back, in case readers have forgotten Ed Dawson's role in the November 3, 1979 events in a Greensboro housing project known as Morningside Home, when a group of Klansmen and Nazis opened fire on a Communist-sponsored anti-Klan demonstration. Five were killed and nine wounded.

Eddie Dawson spat the words out: "You Communist bastard. You asked for the Klan and you got 'em." Paul Bermanzohn was stunned. The man glaring down at him from the passenger side of the tan pickup truck was the same man with whom he had talked amiably just two days earlier, following a Communist Workers Party news conference on the steps of the Greensboro Police Department. Bermanzohn had spoken about the rise of the Klan, the need for militant counteraction, and the upcoming "Death to the Klan" march his group was sponsoring. The man had seemed interested, although he expressed some surprise that there was still such a thing as the Klan in 1979.

From Sharecropper to Landowner

Nat Williamson was a sharecropper when the Great Depression hit the nation. Greensboro was not spared, but Nat worked hard and provided for his family as best as he could. In 1938, Williamson was the first African American in the United States to receive a loan under the new Tenant

Daughter of Nat Williamson.

Purchase Program. This money allowed him to purchase his own farm of almost one hundred acres. According to a granddaughter, the family farmed just about everything:

> *Tobacco and lots of vegetables. When we were growing up, the only thing we bought from the store was like sugar and salt and coffee. Everything else was grown or made. We raised pigs and chickens. My grandfather grew sugarcane and made molasses. We had an apple orchard. He sold butter and eggs, apple cider, vegetables, watermelons and peaches. He had a farm stand in the summer.*

Other rehabilitation clients—farmers in the rural areas of Greensboro—received U.S. Farm Security Administration loans. They were then able to plow their own fields and build their own barns.

Grandmother of tenant farm family.

Sons of rehabilitation client.

"WHAT DID I SAY?"

In 1963, approximately three hundred female students from Bennett College were arrested for sit-ins at Greensboro lunch counters by officers of Greensboro. Jails had already filled quickly, so the deserted polio hospital was chosen to incarcerate the overflow of female arrests. The hospital had been closed for some time. On Sunday afternoon, the women crowded to the windows to hear a speech by Jesse Jackson. Knighton Stanley, campus minister at A&T, recalls Jackson's cutting-edge impact:

> *It was a marvelous speech. Extremely articulate. Extremely knowledgeable. He was on point every step of the way in this speech. It flowed. It was poetic. And it was a marvelous thing…So after the little rally, the gathering was over, we rushed to Jesse and we said, "Jessie, this is a marvelous speech…and we've got to get with you now so we can record it and write it down because this is the kind of speech that you want to publish and to keep."*
>
> *And Jesse looked at us and he was quite surprised and he said, "What did I say?" He had no sense of the impact of that speech, the wisdom of it. And at that moment, he apparently had no recall. I would judge that he did have recall for the speech but since that was perhaps the first speech of that kind that he had ever given, he had no sense of its importance, the gravity of it in terms of a very historic moment not only in the life of the Greensboro movement, but in his own life.*
>
> *Jesse was not talking about the issues or the harshness of being in prison doing without soap and toothpaste. But he dealt with nitty gritty issues of justice. And what this movement meant in terms of it being a turning point in the history of the nation. He said it in historic context and wasn't complaining about being in jail.*

Ruth Pearl Mann recounts her experience with sit-ins at S&K and Roses lunch counters, where blacks were refused service, and her subsequent incarceration in the old polio hospital:

> *When we began the sit-in…I can remember my parents seeing me on T.V. as we were being hauled off to the old polio hospital because all the jails were full. The mayor even issued a statement to the police declaring that if any of us were harmed then they would be fired…I felt as though God was ready to lead his people into a new day where we could all be viewed as people and not colors.*

Judge A's Tongue Lashings

Judge Elreta Mellon Alexander-Ralston of Greensboro was elected a state district court judge in 1968. From the bench, she combated wickedness in unique ways, according to Jim Schlosser's column in the *News & Record*:

> *She invented "Judgment Day," in which she deferred prosecution and dismissed charges against those who had stayed out of trouble for a certain time or completed community service. She threatened to jail county commissioners because of conditions in the courthouse and jail. She rendered lesser verdicts to speeders to prevent insurance companies from raising rates. In 1974, she freed a scalper at the NCAA Final Four in Greensboro because she said police didn't bother scalpers at rock concerts. She once glared at a college professor with a Ph.D. and asked, "Are you a nut?" The professor had pulled a fire alarm, emptying the courthouse. He told Judge A he was exercising his right of political protest to show support for the Communist Workers Party, after five participants were killed during the party's "Death to the Klan" march in 1979. Alexander exercised her authority by sending the professor to a state hospital for psychiatric evaluation. In court, her tongue-lashings left defendants shaking. Her trademark words of address were, "Darling, the truth shall set you free," and…some defendants took her literally and spilled their guts, only to be carted off to jail.*

Judge A's flamboyant, fierce and unforgettable style was reflected in her dress, the click of her heels in the hallways and her lifestyle, as "she walked into court with a full-length mink coat on and a hat, and everyone shut up." She never drove herself but always had a driver. One true happening still circulating Greensboro is this story:

> *A white woman, who mistakenly thought Alexander was white, whispered that she feared her runaway daughter was with "colored boys."*
>
> *"Darling, have you looked at your judge?" the judge responded.*

According to one report, "She recognized that an inordinate number of black children were being brought to the courthouse and charged with petty crimes and getting convicted—while smaller numbers of white kids were showing up…She reasoned that giving youthful offenders a chance to mend their ways meant they wouldn't be saddled for life with a criminal record."

Once, a white Eagle Scout, who had stolen from a store—on a dare from his buddies—went before Judge A. She allowed the young man he could plead "not guilty" if he would fulfill the following requirements:

> *You have to go to your high school and in a seminar confess to all the students what you did and tell them about the court system. You have to visit the jail and see a cell. You have to write a long dissertation about what you are going to do with your life and how this would affect it. In some cases you have to do volunteer work…Then you have to come back on judgment day. If you have done all the things you were supposed to do, then I will enter a verdict of not guilty, and if you haven't done those things, then you might see the jail.*

The judge called it "a prayer for verdict continued."

Alexander-Ralston, the first black woman in the nation elected to the bench, died in 1998. Her portrait now hangs in the Guilford County Courthouse Courtroom 2A, named in her honor.

PART V

Naughty in a Playful Way

Bosomy Display, but No Ankle Showing!

Women of old Greensborough wore a homespun and whalebone-stiffened loose-fitting chemise of linen and over that a laced jacket that nipped their bodies in at the waist. A wooden support up the front forced the female to stand straight and tall. Over these foundation garments, milady wore a crinoline petticoat and hoop underskirt. Her blouse was a tightly fitted basque with high or drop-shouldered neckline, and she wrapped a shawl around her shoulders.

An account of an 1880s wedding took on a wicked tone as Mrs. Virginia Brown Douglas described the bride and her attendants:

> *The occasion was a church wedding in which the bosomy display of bride and lovely bridesmaids was such as would not be allowed in the church today. And the ruffles, without visible means of support, hung perilously low off the shoulders. We spectators…gasped and breathed a sigh of relief when the ceremony was over, the bride resoundingly kissed by the minister, and all floated safely out. It was all right, though, for hands were properly covered by long kid gloves*

> *and not an ankle showed; hardly more than the tip of a toe under the swirling flounces.*

SKILLFUL INTUITION AND TIMELY ANNOUNCEMENT

On a hot Sunday morning in August 1907, Mr. Williams was holding a service in the little wooden church (Presbyterian Church of the Covenant) with all the windows opened. Attending the meeting was Dr. Thomas R. Little, an elder in the church, who had driven up and tied his horse, still hitched to the buggy, to a tree along the street. The horse was visible to Mr. Williams as he stood in the pulpit. During a comprehensive prayer, the vigilant minister noticed that the bridle rein was unfastened and Dr. Little's horse was walking away. What was he to do? Obeying the biblical injunction to "watch and pray," the pastor paused in his prayer and announced over bowed heads, "Dr. Little, your horse is loose!" As the physician ran out of the church, the minister continued his prayer.

RENTING CHURCH PEWS AND OTHER CHURCH RECORDS

In 1820, when Reverend Eli Caruthers became the second minister of Buffalo Church, the oldest charter of any kind in the city of Greensboro, his salary was $250 a year; the church had difficulty raising that amount. The emergency was handled in this way: "A plan to rent the 70 church pews to its members was adopted. Fees for these pews ranged from $6 for those at the front of the church to $1 for those at the back. The first year of such collection showed money to spare; but after that, the idea worked so poorly that the pastor's salary was reduced to $200."

The growth and spirit of Greensboro churches has not been free from interferences, from without and within:

> *While the early churches often used the same meeting places and churches were loaned to congregations of different faiths for special occasions, yet, when it came to church discipline and interdenominational jealousy, none*

could point an accusing finger at the other. The church records are dotted with instances of backsliding, indifference, drunkenness, unfaithfulness, gambling, dancing, card-playing, and other one-time vices among the members.

"Longs" or "Shorts"?

Joe Reece, editor of the *Greensboro Record* until his death in 1915, "brought the news to Greensboro folks, even though such news was often the proverbial 'needle in a haystack' of advertisements." Citizens chuckled at his seasonal warnings as to when the ladies should change their lingerie and the men should abandon their "longs" or "shorts" as the case might be: "It's time to take 'em off" or "It's time to put 'em on," he would announce laconically.

Jovial Comeback: All in a Day's Work

When Moses and Caesar Cone foresaw the need for printed fabrics, they established the Proximity Print Works. They sent new manager J.E. Harden and plant overseer H.A. Barnes to purchase new cloth-printing machinery in Providence, Rhode Island. Harden and Barnes were asked by Rhode Island machinists, "What in the world are you going to do with a printing works way down there in the sticks?" Caesar Cone paid no attention to the snide comment because he firmly believed in Harden and Barnes's abilities—that is, until the first printed fabric was examined by Cone. He reportedly said, "That's fine, boys, but you've printed the cloth on the wrong side." That mistake was corrected immediately, and the Proximity Print Works quickly became the first successful cloth printing plant in the South.

Two Hound Pups and Squire Adam's Hat

In the late nineteenth century, land in Greensboro was purported to be "not of great value nor were those who bought and sold land careful about defining boundaries in deeds," as indicated by this historical fact:

> *It was not uncommon for boundary indications to be trees, stumps, or the like. A deed recorded on May 1, 1879, by "Jas. M. Morehead from Eugene Morehead* et ux*" though obviously couched in terms of humor and affection, might have been well-nigh serious as to the price of the land.* That the parties of the first part for and in consideration of their natural affection for the part of the second part, two hound pups, five dollars and a game cock and two pullets…do bargain and sell to the said Jas. M. Morehead…a parcel or lot of land in Greensboro, bounded as follows: Beginning at a gum stump.

Wicked humor abounds in an 1853 *Greensboro Patriot* article about the Greensborough Mutual Fire Insurance Company's prosperity:

> *About twelve months ago, more or less, we made a blunder in disclosing the whereabouts of the Greensboro Mutual Fire Insurance Company—to wit: that it was in Squire Adam's hat. But the time has now come to repair damages…the concern has grown from a hat-full to a house-full…Having largely outgrown the venerable old bell-crown, the office now requires for its accommodation one of the best business rooms in town.*

Wicked Inflation

Housewives who shopped for groceries in Greensboro in 1874 paid the following prices:

> *Beef—8 to 10 cents*
> *Apples—50 to 75 cents per bushel*
> *Bacon—14 to 15 cents per pound*
> *Hams—17 to 20 cents per pound*
> *Chickens—12 to 20 cents each*

1869 Hotel Breakfast "Feast"?

According to one historical record, the Southern Hotel at 112 West Street had a large bell hanging from the second-story gallery to summon guests to their three meals each day:

> *This hotel was famous through the whole section for the excellence of its meals. Dining there was quite fashionable with the early citizens although many believed that it was unusually extravagant as the hotel charged 50 cents for a meal instead of the 25 cents that the others were content with.*
>
> *In 1869, John and Anna Collins spent the night at the Southern Hotel and were served a breakfast of "rye coffee, stewed squirrel, fried fish, and hot rolls."*

PART VI
Factories, Mills and Businesses

Merchants

The *Greensboro Record* described in 1940 an unknown side of the 1890s business code of ethics:

> *Merchants of that period regarded every other as a rascal or scoundrel. The word ethics was still in the dictionary but its meaning had never been looked up. If you would misrepresent the goods of your competitor and create public distrust, it was considered fine business. Many merchants up and down the streets were not on speaking terms. If a customer owed a debt and wouldn't pay, it was all right to recommend the customer as a good one to some other merchant. In fact, it got so that when a customer was said to be a good risk, it was a question of whether to trust the one recommending or the customer.*

Depression

During the Great Depression, the United Bank & Trust Company at first held on during "hard times," but a steady, though quiet, "business as usual" ceased. According to records, this is what happened:

> *On December 30, 1931, when its doors did not open for business, many of the depositors were literally stunned, for money was scarce and there were bills to be paid; but when they were approached with a plan for reopening the bank, they exhibited their faith and rallied to the cause. Within 6 months after it had closed, its successor, The United Bank and Trust Company, was doing business in Greensboro. It would be difficult to describe the wave of shock which swept over Greensboro when after about 7 months of operation, without warning its doors were closed again, this time forever. That was on February 8, 1933. Many families had just deposited their monthly checks; and with the Great Depression stalking every street, there were many hungry and financially embarrassed people in Greensboro that February.*

Franklin Delano Roosevelt became president on March 4, 1933, and two days later he declared what we know today as the Banking Holiday, "in order to prevent the export, hoarding, or embarking of gold or silver coin, or bullion or currency, or speculation in foreign exchange." This proclamation remained in effect until banks were proven to be solvent.

SHORT-TERM WALKOUTS AND PICKER STICKS

Strikes by millworkers "occupied a prominent place in the lore of the early mills," assert the authors of *Like a Family: The Making of a Southern Cotton Mill World.* Interestingly, many details remain sketchy because local Greensboro newspapers rarely mentioned short-term walkouts. One particular incident, however, was recalled by Lacy Wright and recorded when he and other World War I coworkers attempted to persuade Cone Mills not to lower their piece rates. Mr. Wright recalls what happened:

> *Everybody got worked up about it. They said, "We're going to shut it down. We're going to get old man Tom Gardner down here and talk to us, and if he don't raise the price of the hank, we ain't running no speeders." So he come on down there and talked to us. He said, "No, absolutely not. We're not going to do one thing. You can take it or you can leave it."*

> *Some of the fellows cursed pretty badly, and they said, "Well, by God, we're going to leave." And they walked out and I walked out with them. There wasn't no organization, it was each man making up his mind what he was going to do. We stood around and talked a little bit and all of them said: "Well, by God, let them fire us. We'll just go somewhere else and get us a job." A few hours after the speeder hands walked out the whole plant shut down. Lacy and his father set out to find other jobs. The first group of mills they tried had no openings—Lacy figured that Cone officials had already alerted neighboring mills not to hire striking workers…When Lacy returned to get his belongings, the company decided to offer the strikers more money and they all returned to work.*

Welfare programs for millworkers ultimately proved to be positive, although motives were sometimes questionable. Historians have noted that promoters encouraged village flower shows, sewing clubs and recreation "to secure an attachment for the village to decrease the migratory tendency" and to "not only convert raw cotton into a fine finished product, but of vastly greater importance…discover and covert raw, crude human material…into a prosperous, happy industrious citizenship."

Spoolers, where the yarn is wound from bobbins onto spools. White Oak Cotton Mills.

Left: Speeders, where two strands are drawn and twisted together. White Oak Cotton Mills.

Below: Drawing frames, where five strands are drawn into one. White Oak Cotton Mills.

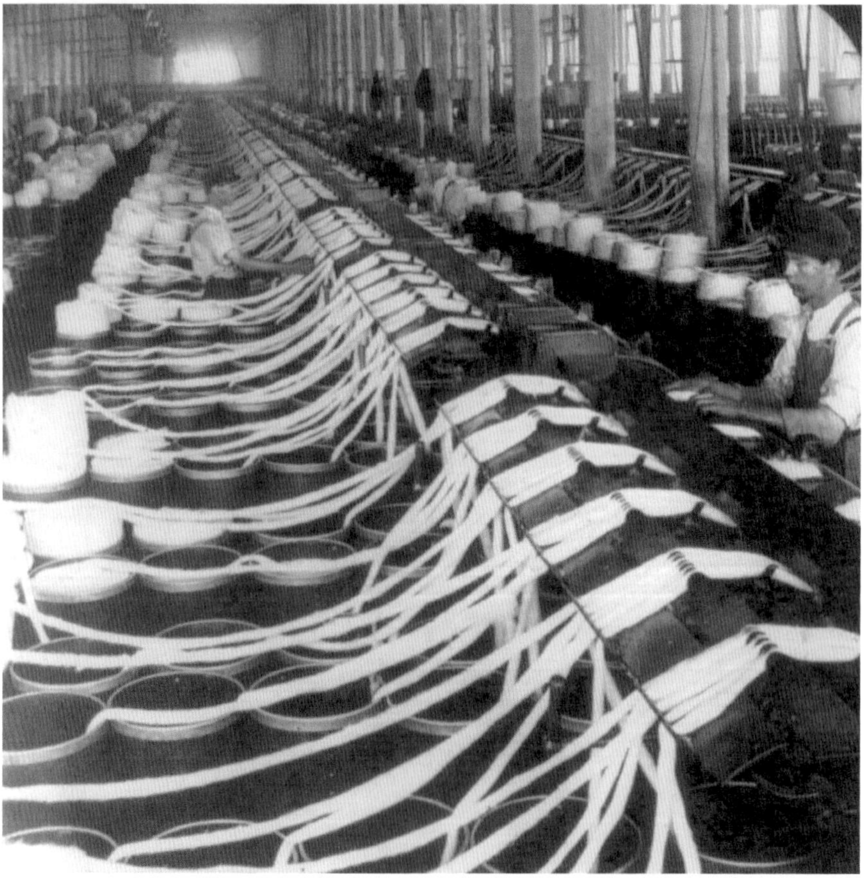

The dye house, where the yarn is dyed, washed and dried. White Oak Cotton Mills.

The book *Like a Family* uses the welfare agents at Greensboro's Proximity Mills in 1903 as an example:

> *These young ladies establish themselves in the heart of the village. A club house, a mill tenement, a room over the company's store, or other convenient quarters are given over to them and becomes the nucleus of their work…They organize social clubs, give parties and entertainments… picnics and ice cream suppers…They visit every family in the village and form close, personal friendships…They make the new families in the village feel at home; visit the sick, and look after the poor. In short welfare agents set themselves up as the arbiters of village life.*

Above: Beaming frames, where threads are straightened for looms. White Oak Cotton Mills.

Left: Spinning room with sixty thousand spindles. White Oak Cotton Mills.

> *New conflicts sometimes arose between parents and children because wage labor in the mills often enticed children of farmers to leave their work in the fields and find public employment. Parents needed and wanted their children to stay at home and work in the fields. Charles Foster went to Greensboro to find work with the railroad so he could live on his own. He relates this incident:*
>
> *"I come back home and told Dad about it, and he said, 'You ain't going to take that. You're too young, you belong to me.' I said, 'Yes, that's right, but I can make my own money, Daddy.' He said, 'Well, you ain't going to make none, because I'll forbid them paying you if you go.' So that knocked that in the head."*

According to mill historians, "Parents considered their children's earnings a family resource, not individual income. A federal report estimated that in 1907—8 girls over the age of fifteen surrendered 89 percent of their earnings to the family while boys of the same age turned over 73 percent."

Strikes affected most mill families in serious ways. Hunger was number one on the list. A correspondent for the *Greensboro Daily News* published the following article about the lack of food:

> *At the outset of the strike, workers had waived their right to union benefits; nevertheless, the UTW* [United Textile Workers] *attempted to provide minimal support by distributing supplies through mill village commissaries. Strikers complained, however, that the commissaries had "chiefly flour, meal, bread, pork and such staples." The union could provide no milk, and as the summer growing season neared an end, millhands' supply of fresh vegetables would soon be depleted. Among many in North Carolina there was "fear of pellagra," and by early August rumblings of "discontent" and "desperation" began to shake the union ranks.*

Lacy Wright, who worked at the Cone family's White Oak plant in Greensboro, recalls picker sticks, "big old wooden sticks about half the size of a ball bat," which mill employees used to beat strikers:

"They brought big boxes of new picker sticks up there and put them in the weave room at Greensboro's White Oak plant," Dodson recalled. "And they told us, 'Now if them flying squads goes to sticking their head in them windows, start cracking heads, and the company'll stand behind you.'" While employees armed themselves, the National Guard lined up outside the mill. "Whenever they thought the flying squad was going to break the National Guard's line, the captain says, 'Anybody crosses the line, shoot him down.' That's what kept them out."

Wright was instructed by his overseer to "go out the door and get you a picker stick." Wright replied, "In place of going out of that side of the building and getting me a picker stick, I'm going back on this side and find me a hole. I'm going out of here." What, at that moment, was on Lacy's mind? "I'll tell you what I thought, at that time. I didn't say much about it, because I couldn't afford to. I thought if them people were that interested in getting them a better situation where they worked, that they were willing to get out and go somewhere to try to shut somebody else down, even if they had to fight about it, that they must have something that we didn't already have. That's exactly what my thoughts was."

In the 1940s, Lacy Wright joined a fight for a union contract at the Cone family's White Oak plant in Greensboro. His heath declined, and he stated, "I noticed when I was young that the cotton dust bothered me," he recalled. "But, of course, I didn't realize what it could do." When he was sixty-one, Lacy retired from the mill because, according to him, "I just couldn't breathe anymore." He was rewarded with a pension of fourteen dollars a month. In 1975, Wright was diagnosed with byssinois, or brown lung. He helped organize the Carolina Brown Lung Association (CBLA) and became president of its Greensboro chapter.

FROM HARASSED MILL SPOOLER TO MINISTER'S WIFE

George Swinney moved to Greensboro in 1920 and worked as a doffer in the Pomona Cotton Mill. Etta Gay Dalton had experienced a hard childhood. She recalled that she "never did know anything but work.

Housework, mostly…You had to get out and milk cows when the snow was above your knees. I just filled the place of a servant." Etta Gay, feeling threatened by her guardian, left because, in her words, "He wasn't married at that time and I could sense he was gonna ruin my life. You know, the Bible says, a virtuous woman, her price is far above rubies. But that was in my heart. I didn't want to go that way. So I left home. I didn't know where I'd go, where I'd wind up. I must have been about fifteen." She traced one of her sisters to Greensboro and joined her there. Through her brother-in-law, Etta Gay got a job spooling at the Pomona Cotton Mill, where she met George Swinney. In 1921, George and Etta Gay married. Historians reveal George Swinney's rough reputation:

> *People who remembered Swinney in those early years in Pomona remembered him as a man who liked a drink and a good time. He was a promising ballplayer; he hunted and fished and loved to play practical jokes. Although his "rough" reputation might have been exaggerated later to accentuate the extent of his conversion, Robert Latta, who grew up in the mill village and later became a minister himself, laughingly recalled, "I never heard him say much about his life before he became a Christian, but I can imagine. He was the type of person that whatever he went at he would have gone at it all the way. And if he were living a life that was not Christian, I can imagine he went all the way there, too."*

In 1927, Swinney felt a call to the ministry. For three more years he and his family lived in Greensboro but took the bus to Burlington each Sunday and walked five miles to Glen Hope Church.

Hard to Be Broke

On February 12, 1938, the following letter signed only with the initials D.B. from Greensboro, North Carolina, was sent to Mrs. Eleanor Roosevelt, Washington, D.C. Mrs. Roosevelt was twice a visitor to Greensboro for several days:

Dear Mrs. Roosevelt

On January 1st I was layed off from my work leaving my father the whole support of our family. Just recently he was cut down to three days a week with a cut in salary. With seven of us in the family it is just about impossible for us to live on this amount.

My mother has been sick for over two months having had a nervous breakdown and we are unable to buy or furnish her with the medicine required for her recovery.

I am 18 years of age the oldest girl in the family, and it just seems impossible for me to get a job any where. I have been to Mills, Stores and Firms of all sorts. I am willing and able to work. Can furnish excellent references but at this time of the year it just seems impossible to find work.

We are so in debt and each week the bills are piling higher and higher that it just seems as if there was no way out.

We must make a pay ment [sic] *on our furniture bill. And if it isn't paid soon they will be out any day for our furniture. And on top of this we are behind in our rent.*

It would be a big help if we could get some of our bills paid on as they are already impatient for their money.

If you could help us out with from $35.00 to $50.00 I believe we would be the happiest family in the world.

We have a good respectable family, none of us have ever been in any trouble, and our characters are above reproach.

Just as soon as I get back to work and the family on their feet again I will pay you back as much a week as possible until your kind favor has been fully repaid.

My father's work has been very poor for the past year. He is an advertising salesman, and his work right now is practically nothing; and as he has had kidney trouble for some time, taking more than he could make, for medicine. He has been improving recently, since he had his teeth extracted, and is looking forward to a job but which will not be available for a month or more. We went through the depression without asking for relief. I registered January 14th for unemployment compensation, and although promised $6.25 a week, have not received a cent as yet.

Won't you please grant me the afore mentioned favor, please make it a personal favor, Mrs. Roosevelt, for if you would refer it to a local agency, I would suffer untold delay and embarrassment.

Altough [sic] *we are poor, we try to hold off embarrassment, for you know it is "hard to be broke, and harder to admit it."*

Please grant me this favor and I will ever be

Gratefully yours,
D.B.

Mrs. Roosevelt's secretary acknowledged Miss B's request on February 15, 1938. Mrs. Roosevelt regretted that she was not able to lend her the money. She had already received many demands on her resources and found it too impossible to respond to so many requests for loans. Mrs. Roosevelt suggested that D.B. go to the National Youth Administration and the United States Employment Service, Department of Labor.

Three-Day Battle over Wages

In the spring of 1969, the story of this battle spread quickly. According to one historian, this is what happened:

It began in December 1968 with cafeteria workers striking at A&T (North Carolina Agricultural and Technical College) in Greensboro. Paid less than the legal minimum wage, the cafeteria workers had neither rights nor benefits, and when they were forced to work overtime, all they got was straight-time pay. Symbolizing the oppression most endured, the strikers got full support from the black community in Greensboro. An organization called GAPP (Greensboro Association of Poor People), known for fighting slum landlords, rallied the black community, churches, and small stores to support the strikers. Nelson Johnson, a leader of GAPP and student at A&T, organized a cafeteria boycott so successful that only five students out of 4,000 crossed the picket line.

The A&T cafeteria strike took place as a wave of black consciousness swept across the country. In Greensboro, activists ran a slate of revolutionary-minded blacks for student leadership positions, including Nelson Johnson at A&T and Claude Barnes at Dudley High School. But after young Claude Barnes was elected president of the student body, school officials refused to seat him. A protest that began as a legal picket to seat Claude ended in an armed confrontation. Enraged at the students' three-day picket, police busted it up, tear-gassing the students and throwing some of them into police cars. Hurling rocks, the students defended themselves, and then 100 of them marched to A&T to ask for some help.

These actions apparently were only the prelude to what would follow:

"With red, watery eyes and torn clothing, the Dudley students appealed to us," Nelson said. "College youth joined them and we marched back to the high school 500 strong, like a liberation army. The school was still in session, but when those students saw us, they abandoned their classes, charging out to join our demonstration."

Although Nelson was arrested for "disrupting a school," the students' demonstration became more and more massive. Declaring a state of emergency, the mayor imposed a curfew. But that night, white Klan-types drove by A&T shooting. Black students returned the fire, and the mayor called in the National Guard. During the night, Willie Grimes, an A&T student, was killed by a bullet in the back of his head. The military battle raged for the next three days. Four hundred A&T students were Vietnam veterans, far more skilled than the cops and National Guard. The students won a decisive military victory, wounding eight cops, while only three students were injured. "We started talking about revolution after that," stated Nelson Johnson, "because there was just no way we could live under this rotten system any longer."

MORE OR LESS TRAPPED

Parental discipline was thought to be essential for family survival on farms and in mills and factories. More times than not, the discipline was extremely harsh and demanding. Through various oral histories, historians have recorded specific incidents:

Walter Vaughn was typical in remembering that his father "made you walk the chalk line. He whipped my brother when he was nineteen years old. Took a strap and tore him up. You done what he said do. You talk back to him, you were tore all to pieces." In the mill village, as in the countryside, this kind of discipline was important to family survival. A family's fate depended on cooperation, and it was essential that children learn at an early age to subordinate their individual desires to the larger interests of the group. But under the new conditions of life and labor, such discipline could leave memories of harsh treatment and deprivation.

Mack Duncan remembered, "I weren't any different than anybody else. When I went to work, my daddy always got all my pay. And money I made went to him automatically." Some parents gave their children part of their wages as an allowance or bought them small presents, but that did not prevent many children from harboring a secret feeling of unfair treatment. One child mill worker reminisced, "We worked five days and a half, ten hours [a day]*," she recalled, "and just made five dollars and a half a week. Mama would take it all but fifty cents. We felt like it wasn't right, but we didn't say nothing; we knowed better. She had three young'uns to raise."*

Child labor legislation.

Many mill-working children tried to escape that hard life by getting married, which historians refer to as a passage marking the transition into "adulthood and independence." Sadly, this might be construed as the old southern idiom "Jumping from the fireplace into the fire," as illustrated by several women's recollections:

> *"I didn't consider myself as grown 'til I married," recalled Edna Hargett. "I was a grown person and I was my own boss then. I knowed Daddy couldn't fuss with me and scold me like he used to." But the newlyweds soon discovered that marriage and parenthood were more confining than anything they had experienced as children. "I just think you just more or less get trapped," observed Eva Hopkins. "My husband and I got married, and we started having babies, and you just have to go on from there. You're just more or less trapped in the job you're in, because when you have children you can't quit and go looking for something else." As a child she had dreamed that marriage would set her free, but the realities of mill work left her with only the hope that her children might have a better life. "I daydreamed when I was young. Before I was married, I would daydream about who I was going to marry. I was going to marry somebody that was rich so that I wouldn't have to work; I could have a nice home and beautiful clothes. Then, after I married, I still had daydreams. And after I had my children, I still had daydreams. I dreamed of wanting a better life for them. It's been a good life, but I'd dreamed of wanted a better life for them…for them not to have to work in the mills, to live in better sections of town, to have nicer homes, more conveniences, nicer cars, nicer every than we had. Dreams like that."*

According to historians, "mill fathers often escaped the difficulties of work and family life in the company of other men." Strong drink helped men forget their worries, as illustrated by Ruth and Jesse Elliot's lives:

> *He got so he was a periodic alcoholic. He would stay sober about three weeks, and in those three weeks he was the best thing; he was the soberest man in town with a vest on. He was a good worker when he was sober. Jesse was so utterly good when he was sober. I reckon that's the only*

> *reason I tolerated him at all. But about once a month he pulled a week's drunk, and he'd drink 'til he couldn't hold any more. And then he'd be sick two or three days. It kind of made me bitter. I couldn't count on Jesse for anything. So I just lived from day to day. I didn't have decent clothes to wear, and the kids,* [their] *clothes were just used—donated. Well, that's no way to live...I've often wished I was a man, because I thought I could change the situation a little bit, and maybe sometimes when Jesse would make me good and mad I'd wish I was a man like him just so I could beat the tar out of him. But I think it's entirely stupid to keep butting your head against a stone wall. I don't care how much I'd want to be a man; there's nothing I can do about it; I'm not a man. I said it's like a woman getting pregnant; it didn't care whether she wanted to have that baby or not, there wasn't much choice about it. She was going to have that baby.*

Although women's lives were difficult, they found solace in the village life, networking with other females. They supported one another through crises, welcomed babies to the world and organized "poundings" with gifts of food and clothing and volunteering to sit up all night, taking turns to offer medicine and comfort to the ill. They also strongly believed that all children of the village should be cared –and even disciplined—for by other mothers. The effort definitely "took a village to rear a child."

Cone Revolution Mill Leaflet for Women

The Revolution Organizing Committee, known as the ROC, met secretly, at first, to attempt to build a union at Greensboro's Cone Revolution Mill. According to one published report, the ROC publicly opened the union drive in April 1977 with a mass meeting, and this is what happened: "Cone management bed-baited and race-baited the union activists, saying the union was being manipulated by communists and was only interested in black workers. But 180 workers boldly came to the mass meeting, sending shivers down Cone management's spines."

The ROC urged oppressed female workers to join the union. The group issued the following leaflet, presented verbatim in its entirety:

WOMEN WORKERS AT CONE MILLS
Everybody who works at Cone Mills has it tough. That's no secret. It's also no secret that women *WORKERS AT Revolution and other Cone Mills plants face a lot of* special *problems that make things even tougher. We can begin to turn this situation around only by organizing to fight now and to struggle to build a strong union*

SUPERVISORS: KEEP YOUR HANDS TO YOURSELVES
One big headache for women workers all over the mill is supervisors making passes at them, pestering them to go out with them, etc. Some of these women have even told certain women, "don't worry about making your eight hours here if you'll just..." There's a big difference *between men workers doing this kind of stuff and* men supervisors *doing it, because supervisors always have the threat of harassment or firing to use if women don't go along or at least keep quiet about it. And although this stuff is bad enough with white women, with black women the supervisors are downright* outrageous. *In fact, the same guy in the Card Room who has been calling white union supporters "nigger-lovers" is well known for his roaming hands and slimy personal questions to black women!*

Of course Herman Cone will claim that this doesn't go on. He'll say: "if you have a complaint, take it to your overseer and he'll straighten everything out." But we know better. In the spinning room a young woman worker reported to the overseer that one supervisor kept making passes at her. What did the overseer do? He laughed at her!

A lot of women are angry about this kind of stuff. But some women just try to play along with the supervisors, laugh them off, and hope they'll go away and leave them alone. The ones that don't give in get harassed and the company covers up for bossmen. Here's on example:

There is one supervisor in the Card Room, Jay Via *who is notorious for this kind of stuff—he's known all over the mill for the* dog *that he is. He had been trying to get next to a young white woman worker for months, when she finally got fed up, she went to the overseer, complained about it, and asked for a transfer to another mill to get away from this creep. She did not get the transfer and she continued getting the same dirty spare help job. She finally quit work—but the supervisor is still here doing the same old dirty thing, and the company covered the whole thing up.*

Women Workers Should Not Have to Put Up with This Garbage to Hold Onto Their Jobs!!

Women who are getting abused like this should know that it's happening to lots of people, *not just them. When you get harassed like this you can stand up and fight it. Tell the ROC and the workers in your department. File a grievance against the supervisor and the ROC will help push this and organize fighting support for you. It is by all workers uniting behind women who get harassed that we will put a stop to all this junk.*

APPENDIX

Recipes Probably Served in Old Greensborough

In an 1847 issue of the *Greensborough Patriot*, nineteen recipes for corn bread were printed. Four years later, thirty-eight recipes for corn bread appeared in the same newspaper. In 1866, one Greensboro restaurant menu offered thirty-seven differently prepared meat dishes at one meal; not one vegetable was available for diners.

Golden Corn Bread

1¼ cups sifted all-purpose flour
¾ cup yellow cornmeal
2–4 Tbs. granulated sugar
4½ tsp. baking powder
1 tsp. salt
1 egg
⅔ cup milk
⅓ cup melted butter, margarine or salad oil

Start heating oven to 425 degrees F. Grease 8" x 8" x 2" pan. Into medium mixing bowl, sift flour, cornmeal, sugar, baking powder, salt. In small bowl, beat egg well with fork; stir in milk, butter; pour, all at once, into flour mixture, stirring with fork until flour is just moistened. Quickly turn batter into greased pan; spread evenly with spatula. Bake 25 to 30 minutes, or until done. Serve hot, cut into squares. Makes 9 servings. For leftover cornbread: Split; butter; then quickly toast under broiler.

Cracklins

1 lb. pork fat

Slice pork into small pieces. For corn bread, cut about ¼-inch square cubes. Fry over medium heat in a cast-iron skillet, stirring often, until golden brown. Drain on paper towels before use.

Cracklin Corn Bread

¼ cup oil or bacon drippings
1½ cups white cornmeal
½ cup flour
1 Tbs. baking powder
¾ tsp. baking soda
½ tsp. salt
dash black pepper
1 cup cracklins (see recipe above)
1 cup buttermilk

Preheat oven to 425 degrees. Pour oil or bacon drippings in cast-iron skillet and heat until hot but not smoking. Combine dry ingredients and cracklins in a mixing bowl. Add buttermilk and mix well. Add heated oil or bacon drippings, leaving about a tablespoon or two in the skillet. Mix well. Pour mixture into hot skillet and bake 20 to 25 minutes until golden brown or wooden pick inserted into center comes out clean.

Prune Bread

1 cup uncooked dried prunes
3 cups sifted all-purpose flour
4 tsp. baking powder
½ tsp. baking soda

1½ tsp. salt
2 Tbs. sugar
¼ cup shortening
2 Tbs. grated orange rind
2 eggs, beaten
1 cup milk

Start heating oven to 350 degrees. Grease 10" x 5" x 3" loaf pan. If prunes are very dry, boil in water to cover, 5 minutes; drain. Pit prunes; put prunes through food chopper, using medium blade. Sift flour, baking powder, baking soda, salt and sugar. Cut in shortening with pastry blender or 2 knives, scissor-fashion, until like coarse cornmeal. Stir in prunes and rind. Combine eggs and milk; add to flour mixture; mix well; turn into pan. Bake 1 hour or until done. Cool in pan 10 minutes; remove. Cool overnight before slicing.

Chipped Beef on Toast

Note: Today dried beef comes in packages or glass jars. To prepare, tear dried beef into medium shreds.
¼ cup butter or margarine
¼ lb. dried beef
3 Tbs. flour
2 cups milk

Melt butter. Add dried beef. Stir in flour. Add milk slowly, stirring. Cook, stirring until smooth and thickened. Serve on toast. Makes 4 servings.

Corn Fritters, Southern Style

1 cup sifted all-purpose flour
1 tsp. baking powder
1 tsp. salt
2 eggs
¼ cup milk
2 tsp. salad oil
2½ cups cooked or canned whole-kernel corn

Sift flour with baking powder, salt. Beat eggs; add milk, 2 tsp. salad oil. Stir in flour mixture and then corn. Drop by tablespoonfuls into fat heated to 365 degrees F. on deep-fat frying thermometer as in shallow frying. Fry 3 to 5 minutes, turning once. Makes 5 or 6 servings.

Spareribs and Sauerkraut

2 to 4 Tbs. fat or salad oil
3 lb. spareribs
2 sliced large onions
1/4 tsp. salt
1/8 tsp. pepper
1/2 cup boiling water
2 to 2 1/2 can sauerkraut
1/4 to 1/2 tsp. caraway seeds
1 grated, pared, cored cooking apple

In hot fat (amount depends on fat on meat) in Dutch oven, sauté spareribs until brown on all sides. Add onions; sauté until tender. Sprinkle with salt, pepper. Add water; simmer, covered, 1 hour. Move spareribs to one side of Dutch oven; place sauerkraut, caraway seeds and apple on other side; cook, covered, 20 to 30 minutes. Season to taste.

To serve: Lift sauerkraut from liquid; arrange on one end of platter. With scissors, cut spareribs into pieces; place on other end of platter. Makes 3 or 4 servings.

Cucumber Sandwiches

2 Tbs. Worcestershire sauce
1/4 cup fresh dill, minced
2 drops Tabasco
3 Tbs. lemon juice
1/4 tsp. salt
3 scallions, minced
1 clove garlic, minced
1 lb. cream cheese

2 loaves white or wheat bread
6–8 cucumbers, thinly sliced

Combine first seven ingredients in food processor. Add cheese in small amounts and blend. Refrigerate for 30 minutes. Cut bread into shapes and spread layer of sauce, topping with thin slice of cucumber.

Fried Pumpkin

1 pumpkin, peeled
½ cup milk
1 egg
salt and pepper
¾ cup flour

Slice peeled pumpkin thin and add pieces in mixture of milk, egg, salt and pepper. Then roll in flour. Fry in oil until brown.

Shrimp Salad

1 lb. boiled shrimp, peeled
¼ cup chopped celery
½ cup chopped onion
3 Tbs. pickle relish
½ cup real mayonnaise
1 tsp. salt

Toss all ingredients and chill. Serve on beds of lettuce

Pumpkin Pie with Pecans

2 eggs, beaten
2 cups mashed pumpkin
⅔ cup sugar
¼ tsp. salt
1 tsp. cinnamon

¼ tsp. ginger
⅛ tsp. cloves
1¾ cups evaporated milk
¼ cup melted butter
1 cup chopped pecans
3 Tbs. half and half
1 cup brown sugar

Mix first 8 ingredients. Pour into prepared deep-dish pie shell. Bake at 425 degrees for about 15 minutes. Reduce heat to 350 degrees and bake for 45 additional minutes. Mix butter, pecans, half and half and brown sugar. Spread over hot pie. Put under broiler for 4–5 minutes. Watch the entire time to prevent burning.

CREAM PUFFS

1 cup boiling water
½ cup Crisco (butter-type Crisco preferred)
1 cup plain flour
4 eggs
1 tsp. salt

Bring water and Crisco to a boil. Add flour. Stir until ball forms in center of pan. Cool. Add unbeaten eggs, beating after each one. Add salt and stir lightly. Line cookie sheets with nonstick baking paper of choice. Drop mixture from spoon (or pastry bag and tube). Bake at 450 degrees for 15 minutes; then reduce oven temperature to 350 degrees and bake 30 more minutes. Cool. Fill with chicken salad, pimento cheese or whipped cream. Makes approximately 24 small puffs or 12 large puffs.

ICED TEA

1½ cups sugar
1 quart water
8 tea bags black tea

Pour the sugar in a 2-quart pitcher. Set aside. Place 1 quart water in large pot on stove top burner set on medium-high heat. Add tea bags to water. Bring water just to the point where small bubbles begin to form around edge of pot. Do not bring to a full boil. Remove from heat and discard tea bags. Pour hot tea in pitcher containing sugar. Mix well until all sugar is dissolved. Add 1 tray or modern-day equivalent of ice cubes. Stir. Add water from tap to bring water level to within 4 inches of the top of pitcher. Refrigerate for 30 minutes.

Cole Slaw

1 large head of cabbage, chopped fine
1 cup chopped green bell pepper
1 cup chopped onion
1 cup white vinegar
1 cup sugar
2 Tbs. salt
¼ Tbs. black pepper
1 Tbs. olive oil or salad oil
2 Tbs. celery seed
¼ cup mayonnaise

Mix chopped cabbage, bell pepper and onion in a large bowl. Set aside. In a small saucepan, bring vinegar, sugar and salt to a boil, stirring until sugar is completely dissolved. Allow vinegar/sugar mixture to cool 5 minutes and then pour over cabbage mix. Stir in black pepper, olive oil, celery seed and mayonnaise. Mix well. Adjust ingredients to taste. If too sweet, add vinegar. If too much vinegar, add sugar and oil. If bland, add salt. Refrigerate for 30–45 minutes. Pour off excess liquid before serving.

Fried Okra

vegetable cooking oil, enough to cover okra completely in frying pan
4 cups cut-up okra
1 egg
1 cup white cornmeal

2 Tbs. flour
½ tsp. salt
½ tsp. black pepper

Heat oil in large frying pan on medium heat. Use a pan large enough not to crowd the okra. Chop okra into 1-inch pieces. Beat egg lightly in a bowl and add the okra. Stir to coat okra with egg and let sit for 5 minutes. Place the cornmeal, flour, salt and pepper in a separate large bowl and mix. Dredge the okra in the cornmeal mix to cover all sides of okra with mix. Place one piece of okra in the hot oil and check that it immediately bubbles and sizzles. If not, the oil is not hot enough. Increase heat until you get the bubbles when adding one piece of okra. If oil temperature is okay, add all the okra. Cook the okra, stirring frequently, until it is one shade from burned. When done, the okra should not be bright green. It should be brown with a few black edges. Place cooked okra on paper towels to absorb some of the oil. It will be crunchy. Serve hot.

Fried Catfish

1 cup white cornmeal
⅓ cup all-purpose flour
2 tsp. salt
1 tsp. black pepper
½ tsp. cayenne pepper
¼ tsp. garlic powder
2 medium eggs
¼ cup buttermilk
catfish fillets, 3 or 4 medium pieces per person
enough cooking oil to cover the fish

Combine all dry ingredients on a plate, mix well. Beat eggs and buttermilk in a medium-size bowl. Wash catfish fillets and pat dry. Dip fillets in the egg wash and shake off excess; then roll in the cornmeal mix to coat thoroughly on all sides. Make sure oil is hot; then place fish in frying pan and fry until golden brown on both sides. Drain on paper towels and serve hot.

Bibliography

All Aces Media. "Award Winning Documentary: Greensboro's Child." vimeo.com/1711003.

"Archibald Debow Murphey." www.rootsweb.ancestry.com/~ncccha/biographies/archibaldmurphy.html.

Arnett, Ethel Stephens. Written under the direction of Walter Clinton Jackson. *Greensboro North Carolina: The County Seat of Guilford.* Chapel Hill: University of North Carolina Press, 1955.

"Benefit of Clergy Legal Definition." legal-dictionary.thefreedictionary.com/benefit+of+clergy.

Bermanzohn, Paul C., and Sally A. Bermanzohn. *The True Story of the Greensboro Massacre.* New York: Cesar Cauce Publishers and Distributors, Inc., 1980.

Bermanzohn, Sally A. *Through Survivors' Eyes: From the Sixties to the Greensboro Massacre.* Nashville, TN: Vanderbilt University Press, 2003.

"The Civil Rights Movement Through the Eyes of a Woman of God." www.glynn.k12.ga.us/BHS/academics/junior/hunt/chassidym23785.

"David Caldwell: 1725–1821." www.therestorationmovement.com/caldwell,david.htm.

"Dear Mrs. Roosevelt: The Letters." newdeal.feri.org/eleanor/db0238.htm.

"Definitions of *Quackery* on the Web." www.google.com/search?hl=en&rlz=1T4ADRA_enUS374US374&defl=en&q=def.

"The 1859 Crisis Over Hinton Helper's Book, The Impending Crisis." litigation-essentials.lexisnexis.com/webcd/app?action=DocumentDisplay&crawlid.

"Families in Colonial North Carolina." www.learnc.org/lp/editions/nchist-colonial/4107.

"Fish Fry—Southern Fried Catfish Recipe." www.olsouthrecipes.com/fishfry.html.

"Frank Lucas (Drug Lord)." en.wikipedia.org/wiki/Frank_Lucas_(drug_lord).

"Frontline: The Long Pilgrimage of Jesse Jackson: Jesse the Orator." www.pbs.org/wgbh/pages/frontline/jesse/impressions/orator.html.

"Furor Over Hinton Helper's Book." www.learnnc.org/lp/editions/nchist-antebellum/4493.

"Greensboro Beautiful Receives Major Gift for Caldwell Park Enhancements." www.greensboro-nc.gov/pressreleases/2000/000531.htm.

"Greensboro Massacre." en.wikipedia.org/wiki/Greensboro_massacre.

Hairston, Otis. L. *Picturing Greensboro: Four Decades of African American Community.* Charleston, SC: The History Press, 2008.

Hall, Jacquelyn Dowd, James Leloudis, Robert Korstad, Mary Murphy, Lu Ann Jones and Christopher B. Daily. *Like a Family: The Making of a Southern Cotton Mill World*. New York: W.W. Norton & Company, 1987.

Hendrick, Burton Jesse, and Woodrow Wilson. *The Life and Letters of Walter H. Page*. Vol. 1. N.p., n.d.

Johnson, Guion Griffis. *Ante-Bellum North Carolina: A Social History*. Chapel Hill: University of North Carolina Press, 1937.

"List of Dead in Tornado-Ravaged Greensboro Swells to 12; Work of Relief and Rehabilitation Speeded." www.gendisasters.com/north-carolina/7793/greensboro-nc-tornado-destruction-ap.

"Locals Remember 1936 Greensboro Tornado." www.digtriad.com/news/features/article.aspx?storyid=121872&catid=216.

Ludwig, Charles. "Levi Coffin: President of the Underground Railroad." www.afgen.com/coffin1.html.

McLauglin, Nancy H. "Black History's Roots Run Deep in the Triad." News-Record.com. www.allvoices.com/…/5311984-black-historys-roots-run-deep-in-the-triad.

"Nat Williamson Family." www.morningsonmaplestreet.com/natwilliamson2.html.

"The 1936 Cordele-Greensboro Tornado Outbreak." en.wikipedia.org/wiki/1936_Cordele-Greensboro_tornado_outbreak.

Nivens, David. "Hometowns Mystery & Scandals." *High Point Enterprise*, July 29, 2010.

"North Carolina: 30th Anniversary of Ku Klux Klan–Nazi Shooting—No One Served a Single Day in Prison for 5 Killings." www.realcourage.org/2009/11/north-carolina-30th-anniversary-of-klan-nazi-shooti.

"O. Henry." en.wikipedia.org/wiki/O._Henry.

"O. Henry (William Sydney Porter)." www.orrt.org/ohenry.

"Platodurham's Weblog." platodurham.wordpress.com.

"Remembering Shalonda Poole: 20 Years Later." www.news-record.com/blog/61601/entry/95013.

Schlosser. Jim. "'Judge A' Flamboyant, Fierce and Unforgettable." News-Record.com: Greensboro & the Triad. www.news-record.com/content/2009/11/02/article/judge_a_flamboyant_fierce_and u.

Seals, Ryan. "Haunted by a Memory and a Murdered." www.news-record.com/content/2008/07/19/article/haunted_by_a_memory_and_a_m.

Sink, Alice E., and Nickie Doyal. *Boarding House Reach: North Carolina's Entrepreneurial Women.* Wilmington, NC: Dram Tree Books, 2007.

"Unsolved Murder of Shalonda Poole, 7 Greensboro, NC 1990—Help Find the Missing." www.helpfindthemissing.org/forum/showthread.php?t=13312.

Waller, Signe. *Love and Revolution: A Political Memoir.* Lanham, MD: Rowman Littlefield, 2002.

"Walter Hines Page." en.wikipedia.org/wiki/Walter_Hines_Page.

Watterson, Kathryn. "Cops and Klan Walked After Greensboro, NC Massacre." *Trenton Times*, February 1996. www.hartford-hwp.com/archives/45a/151.html.

Wheaton, Elizabeth. *Codename GREENKIL: The 1979 Greensboro Killings.* Athens: University of Georgia Press, 1987.

About the Author

Alice E. Sink is the published author of books and numerous short stories, articles and essays in anthologies and in trade and literary magazines. She earned her MFA in creative writing from the University of North Carolina–Greensboro. For thirty years, she taught writing courses at High Point University in High Point, North Carolina, where she received the Meredith Clark Slane Distinguished Teaching/Service Award in 2002. The North Carolina Arts Council and the partnering arts councils of the Central Piedmont Regional Artists Hub Program awarded Sink a 2007 grant to promote her writing.